Penguin Business Library

C000007888

Walter Goldsmith was born in 1938 and educated at the Merchant Taylors School. After qualifying as a chartered accountant he joined Black and Decker Ltd in 1966, where he progressed through various responsibilities to become Managing Director, a European Director and finally Corporate Vice-President and President of the Pacific International Operations, headquartered in Los Angeles. From 1979 to 1984 he was Director General of the Institute of Directors, an international professional body and representational voice for business leaders as individuals. He is currently Chairman of Leisure Development Ltd, a non-executive Director of Bestobell plc, the Lesser Group and BUPA Medical Centre. He is also a member of the British Tourist Authority and was a member of the English Tourist Board from November 1982 until February 1984. He has recently taken up the appointment of Chairman and Chief Executive of Korn/Ferry International Ltd, the UK arm of the world's largest executive search organization.

Walter Goldsmith is married and has four children.

David Clutterbuck is a management journalist and editorial consultant. Formerly managing editor of *International Management*, he contributes to the *Observer*, *The Times*, the *Economist*, *Chief Executive* and a number of other publications in the United Kingdom and abroad. He is editor of several specialist management journals, including *Issues* and *Strategic Alternatives*. His previous books include *How to Be A Good Corporate Citizen* and *The Re-Making of Work*, as well as a book of children's stories, *The Tale of Gribble the Goblin*.

David Clutterbuck is currently chairman of publishers ITEM Ltd. He is married with three sons and lives in Berkshire.

Walter Goldsmith and David Clutterbuck have also published *The Winning Streak* (Penguin).

The Winning Streak
Check Book

Walter Goldsmith
and David Clutterbuck

 Penguin Books

Penguin Books Ltd, Harmondsworth, Middlesex, England
Viking Penguin Inc., 40 West 23rd Street, New York, New York 10010, U.S.A.
Penguin Books Australia Ltd, Ringwood, Victoria, Australia
Penguin Books Canada Limited, 2801 John Street, Markham, Ontario, Canada L3R 1B4
Penguin Books (N.Z.) Ltd, 182–190 Wairau Road, Auckland 10, New Zealand

First published in Great Britain as *The Winning Streak Workout Book* by
Weidenfeld & Nicolson 1985
Published in Penguin Books 1986

Reproduced, printed and bound in Great Britain by
Hazell Watson & Viney Limited,
Member of the BPCC Group,
Aylesbury, Bucks
Typeset in Monophoto Photina

Contents

How to use this book

The Winning Streak Check Book aims to do two things, First, it aims to help you understand how good (or bad) your company is in the critical factors that make for long-term business success – whether, in fact, it has or is developing the winning streak. Second, it aims to help you as a manager or as a chief executive create the winning streak in the operations for which you are responsible.

A large part of this book is devoted to questionnaires. These should not be thought of as a quiz, nor are they some kind of complex psychometric test. Their purpose is solely to help you think through the values and attitudes that make for business success, in the context of your own company. We hope that simply making yourself answer these questions will provide valuable insights into your company. We are pretty sure that honest answers to some of them will embarrass you.

This book is less about insights, however, than about action. All the management analysis and advice in the world is of little value if it does not lead to changes in behaviour, attitude and practice. Following each questionnaire is an action guide, which pursues the themes of the questions to suggest practical steps that you – at whatever level of management you are – can use to develop the winning streak.

NOTE: although managers have been referred to in this book as 'he', this is in no sense intended to exclude the 'she's of the business world, who constitute a regrettably small – 8 per cent – but ever-increasing proportion of managers.

Acknowledgements

Many thanks are due to:

Neville Wills of the Gryphon Group

Roger Hayes of P A Management Consultants

Marion Devine of Clutterbuck Associates

Richard Lamming of Brighton Polytechnic

Fred Buggie of Strategic Innovation International

Introduction: Putting
The Winning Streak into practice

When we finished writing *The Winning Streak* just over a year ago, we hoped that it would stimulate discussion in British boardrooms, among ordinary managers and in business schools. We wanted to create an awareness that British companies can and sometimes do rank with the best in the world, and those that do have achieved this by developing and maintaining a winning streak. We also wanted to encourage other companies to learn from the experiences of the most successful and to develop their own winning streaks.

The first two aims have certainly been achieved to a considerable degree. *The Winning Streak* has become a business best seller and has been launched in the United States with the support of Tom Peters, author of *In Search of Excellence*, who has modified some of the conclusions of his own book as a result. In particular, Peters now places increased stress upon leadership and upon few and simple financial controls. We have discussed our findings with a wide range of business people and academics across the country, satisfying them, we hope, that the basic lessons of the excellence movement are valid in the British context. The third aim has proved rather more elusive. Time and again we have been asked: 'This is all very well for the companies in *The Winning Streak*, but how do we put all this into practice in our companies?' This book is an attempt to bridge that gap.

YOUR PLAN TO WIN

No company, not even the most successful of the companies examined in *The Winning Streak*, is excellent at everything. But the most successful companies are a lot better at all or most of a number of critical skills of their business than other companies are. To achieve that measure of excellence across the board requires a great deal of effort, starting at the top. It requires a well-communicated and comprehensive plan and a very clear idea of how the company rates in all aspects of its behaviour that concern winning.

So where do you start? That depends on who you are. The nature and the degree of the changes that you can achieve will naturally be different between the executive suite and the junior manager's office. So we have deliberately given the practical sections of each chapter two alternating themes: one addressed to the chief executive, and the other to the individual manager. There are, however, many similarities between the two themes. In his own department, and within practical limits, the ordinary manager can be his own chief executive. Learning new habits, attitudes and behaviour now will help his or her future career.

The first step to take in either case is to establish where your company stands now. How does it compare with its competitors in the eight winning characteristics: leadership, autonomy, control, involvement, market orientation, zero basing, innovation and integrity? And what are the 'cultural' factors that help or hinder your company from achieving excellence in each respect?

You can use various methods to compare with the competition. For example, ask customers, employees, suppliers and other more or less informed observers in the Press or the City. Solicit opinions from anyone who can provide an alternative view, and *listen* to what they have to say, even if it is not very palatable. How many times have companies or whole industries collapsed because their top managers held the arrogant assumption that they had an unassailable superiority in the areas that mattered. Consider the Swiss watch industry, and the English watch industry before that. Both assumed that their manifest excellence (manifest to them, that is) in quality and technology was immutable. It hardly occurred to either of them that they could be overtaken by outsiders.

From the chief executive's point of view, an independent survey by a market research organization is likely to elicit the most honest and accurate results. At a more junior level, it is simpler, cheaper and probably as effective to ask people directly. You can search through periodicals to see which aspects of your own operations and those of your competitors receive praise from academics and business journalists. Even if you are sure that the accounts you read greatly exaggerate the excellence of one function or another of a competitor, don't dismiss them as mere public relations hype. Use the public perception that company has as the minimum to which your company should aspire in that characteristic. After all, customer expectations will have been raised, and if you do not meet them someone else will. You can also conduct structured interviews with employees of your company who have been recruited from competitors. Get them honestly to compare the two companies in a fairly detailed report.

All these approaches will provide subjective data. Objective data is harder to acquire. Even if your research gives a clear picture of how good your company is in each characteristic (and very few companies' research does), your competitors are unlikely to make available similar data on themselves. In this case, you may be better advised to ask yourself regarding each characteristic: 'If we were to be the best in the industry in this respect, what would that entail?' Your answer, if sufficiently detailed, can make a pretty good yardstick against which to measure current performance.

The next step is to understand what is preventing your company or your department from achieving the best. There may be physical or financial constraints: it's hard to produce top quality goods on obsolete machinery. These are normal, straightforward management problems that every manager, in theory at least, should be able to tackle, given the resources. (Obtaining the resources may be the difficult bit. You may have to demonstrate the winning streak in other areas before the cash becomes available.) However, far more companies fall down when trying to surmount the invisible, intangible barriers of company culture.

Understanding your company culture   Much has been written about company culture in recent years, most of it unintelligible and of slight practical use, or simplistic and misleading. Rather than risk adding to either of those extremes, we will simply explain how you can begin to gain an insight into the complexities of your company's culture and how, with care and experiment, you can use the positive elements of company culture to reinforce changes of direction.

It probably won't surprise you that the experts are divided as to what company culture is. For our purposes, we shall define it as 'a set of behavioural and attitudinal norms, to which most or all members of an organization subscribe either consciously or subconsciously and which exert a strong influence on the way people resolve problems, make decisions and carry out their everyday tasks'. Inherent in this definition are certain truisms:

● most people are unaware that their behaviour in the organization is conditioned by the culture they have acquired. Yet place them in another familiar organization with a different culture, say the family, the golf club or the local church, and they automatically switch to that organization's cultural norms.

● the culture provides rationality for decisions and behaviour that might appear irrational to the outside world.

● the culture affects everything a company does; it is all-pervasive and therefore very difficult for one individual, even if he is the most powerful person in the company, to change.

● culture does change as new experiences oblige the organization to learn new responses. That change is almost always evolutionary rather than revolutionary. The revolutionary change of culture requires a massive transplant of people with different cultural ideas; but transplants are often rejected, or absorbed and adapted to produce a hybrid, or simply allowed to exist in tandem.

● the culture may not be uniform throughout a large organization. Subcultures can and do establish themselves in departments that regard themselves as somehow different, or in certain layers of the hierarchy. (For example, in many companies the managerial culture requires different – sometimes several different – dress codes. Not only may all managers be required to wear suits rather than casual clothes, but the cut and cost may vary subtly as you progress up the hierarchy.) None the less, these subcultures will normally espouse most of the common values of the general company culture.

You can gain an understanding of the culture of your company in several ways. First, search for the folklore. Have someone collect the stories long-serving employees recount to explain why things are done one way and not another. Look particularly for tales that have overtones of popular mythology. The stories people respond most deeply to and which have most effect upon their behaviour are those they associate with powerful tales of their childhood. Look for Jack the Giantkiller in 'how we took on IBM and won', or for the Ugly Duckling in the turnaround of an ailing unit. Identify your company's own heroes of folklore and what they are revered for. Try to find out what folktales people associate with you. (Get the personnel depart-ment to ask people at different levels as the 'fun' part of a training exercise.)

The power of corporate folklore is far stronger than most managers realize. If you want to change behaviour, it has to be done at a deep, subconscious level as much as at the rational, conscious level. You can make that task easier by appealing to employees' subconscious associations with heroes from the legacy of your company's folklore. Politicians, playwrights and others in the business of influencing people's subconscious make constant use of such associations; so can you.

Of course, the folklore is only a small part of the company culture. To gain an insight into the broader culture you can establish 'culture workshops', where managers are put through exercises designed to expose common attitudes, behaviour and values. Judi Marshall and Adrian McLean of the Centre of Organizational Change and Develop-ment at the University of Bath have conducted such workshops for a number of companies. As they told a management conference at Ashridge:

> A compressed, one-day organization simulation, for example, gives parti-cipants a content-less structure to fill with their own assumptions and values (about organizations and about themselves). Through this exer-cise, participants can live their organization. Watching different groups from the same organization do the simulation, we see core patterns re-peated again and again. ... We are generally unaware of our taken-for-granted world, and most of culture is in this realm.

None of this gives you any prescriptive solutions to the problem of changing culture, but it does make people aware of both the potential and the difficulties of achieving durable change.

We stress the point about durability of change because so much of the effort that top management of companies puts into creating change never penetrates beyond the surface. One important reason for this is that there are in reality two orders of change. The first, say Marshall and McLean,

> ... involves adjustments, say in how one performs one's job, whilst the ground rules, within which one is working, remain the same. For ex-ample, a glass blower may be required to produce a bowl rather than a water jug, but to traditional quality standards and for a select market. ... Second-order change occurs if basic assumptions change. To pursue

our example, the glass blower may now be required to produce for a mass market, and volume rather than quality becomes the key standard of performance. This time a change of behaviour must be accompanied by a different attitude to the task, that may, to the glass blower, represent a radical change.

One major reason, they maintain, that so many organizational development programmes which aim to produce second-order change in fact only produce first-order change is that the programmes do not take sufficient account of the power of the existing culture to maintain the status quo. Another reason is that culture is so insidious that it colours thinking about change, mentally limiting the range of options of those entrusted with the task of implementing change. 'To engage in successful second-order change we need to penetrate to the deep structures of organizational life, and to work at these levels', say Marshall and McLean.

One other way of gaining an insight into your company's culture is by answering the questionnaires in this book.

The more you delve into your company's culture, the more you will realize how unreal many of the overt slogans are. Take 'We are all here to make a profit'. It is an aim we would all instinctively aspire to. But what is the reality? Author Graham Cleverley expressed it well in his book *Managers and Magic* in 1971:

> The fact of the matter is that almost no one in business, judged by what he does, is there to make a profit. For security, yes. For fellowship, yes. For status and self-esteem and power and comfort, yes. But the number of people [in a company] ... whose behaviour is conditioned by the desire to make a profit is probably about equal to the number of people in a Victorian congregation (when Christianity was fashionable) whose behaviour was materially affected by Christ's commandments.

Having gained at least some understanding of your company's culture you can examine whether it helps or hinders the attitudes, values and behaviour you want to establish as normal. Where the culture helps, you have simply to build on what is there already, although that is certainly not as easy as it sounds. Where the culture is plainly a barrier, your choice depends upon the timescale you allow yourself and the amount of effort you are prepared to expend. Controlled evolutionary change is more likely to succeed, but will take a long time and a sustained effort, continually reinforcing new values by example, by reward, and by making people at all levels aware of the culture. Revolutionary change will be much quicker, but will create far greater upheaval, resentment and potential backlash.

That sounds like hard work and it is. But winning rarely comes easily.

An action plan for winning Your next step is to draw up an action plan to create the winning streak in those characteristics where your researches show the largest shortfall, and where your analysis indicates the best potential for commercial gain. The plan should concentrate on a small number of characteristics – three at most – or else the culture shock may leave your subordinates dazed. Putting the same priority on all the winning streak characteristics is inadvisable, because few people will have either the time or the span of attention to deal with them all properly. That doesn't mean you should ignore the other characteristics. Watch them, and keep up a gentle pressure to improve them slowly.

The action plan should define the areas you aim to improve, why they need improvement, and who is to be involved. It should set targets for carrying out information, training and acclimatization exercises, and for levels of excellence to be achieved in, say, production quality or customer service. Wherever possible, these targets should have a numerical element, so that progress can be compared year on year. Action should begin at once, and everyone involved in formulating the plan should agree to a personal set of objectives aimed at creating the winning streak in his or her area of responsibility. These personal objectives include changes in one's own behaviour and values.

None of this will work without the commitment of the mass of people in the company. They need to know what you aim to do, why, how it affects them and what part they can play. They need to be listened to and given the opportunity to influence the cultural change as it occurs. You will almost certainly have to work hard to increase their awareness of the company culture, both as it is and as you intend it to be. Like the psychologist attempting to cure a patient's phobia, you can cure cultural maladies only by bringing them into the open.

As the plan is implemented you must monitor how performance is improving by the criteria you set at the beginning. You should also keep an eye on how the competition is doing – after all, they will probably have read this book too. As one gap is narrowed or filled, move on to the next most critical. Expect and plan for this to be a continuous cycle in which each of the characteristics critical to your winning streak is given a regularly reviewed target, but where only two or three receive special attention at one time.

Above all, make it clear to everyone that everything that is happening is about winning. People like to work for a winner and hate to work for a loser. This is how Michael Naylor, general director of corporate strategic planning at General Motors, expressed it in an article for *Long Range Planning* magazine:

> You must develop and foster YES-I-CAN attitudes. Winners have one thing in common – they have confidence in themselves. They win the competition because, deep inside, they know they can do it. Working to develop a winning attitude in your people is one of the most strategic things you can do. Somebody once said that 'Losers let it happen. Winners make it happen.'

Have you got the courage to create the winning streak?

1 Winning through leadership

The characteristic that emerged from *The Winning Streak* as central to business growth was the quality of a company's leadership. The business leader need not be charismatic (indeed, if he fails to combine charisma with wisdom, disaster is almost inevitable). But he must be able to motivate those around him, to provide a sense of mission for the organization as a whole, and to ensure that all the middle and junior management leaders down the line have clear objectives they can work to, to motivate and direct their own subordinates' efforts. It is no coincidence that leadership is now becoming a popular topic at gatherings of senior executives, nor that acknowledged business leaders are making forthright and controversial comments on the quality of executive leadership in Britain.

If what is being urged appears to be a return to traditional values, that is not surprising. However, the challenge for today's corporation is not just to restore old values but to update them. Before you can attempt to reassert effective leadership, you need to assess whether a real leadership culture exists in your company. One of the best starting points for this kind of analysis is to ask pertinent and challenging questions, such as these below.

GENERAL QUESTIONS

1   From comments in the Press, stockbrokers' reports and so on does your company's top management emerge as ...?

> *dynamic, aggressive and decisive*
> *cautious, low-profile and indecisive*
> *somewhere in between*

2   When did top management in your company last make a decision you would regard as courageous?

within the past month
within the past six months
within the past year
never as far as you can recall

3   Is top management in your company seen as ...?

a team
a collection of disparate individuals

4   In your company is the instinctive response to a crisis ...?

total panic: everyone runs around like headless chickens
a senior manager steps in and takes charge
managers put their heads together constructively, and each takes responsibility for handling part of the solution personally and swiftly

5   If a manager is someone who organizes resources and a leader is someone who motivates other people to get a task done, which would you say predominated in your company ...?

leaders
managers

6   What proportion of employees in general believes that top management in your company knows what it is doing?

two-thirds or more
one-third or more
less than one-third

VISIBLE TOP MANAGEMENT

7   Take a random group of a dozen low-level employees. How many of them would be able to name all the executive directors of the company?

more than half
less than half
none

8   How often does top management visit the shopfloor?

> *every week*
> *every month*
> *every year*
> *never*

9   When top managers do visit the plants or the field, do they ...?

> *come to give a formal (pep) talk to the whole staff*
> *come to talk to managers only*
> *come to look and listen for themselves*
> *come to discuss informally with each and anyone*

10   If the chairman walked through the shopfloor, how many people would recognize him?

> *less than half*
> *more than half*
> *almost everyone*

11   How often does top management personally say 'Thank you' to junior employees?

> *frequently*
> *rarely*
> *never*

12   Does your chief executive personally discover things that need to be remedied at plant/operator level ...?

> *almost daily*
> *every week*
> *every month*
> *every year*
> *never*

13   What proportion of executive meetings take place in the field, where the problem (and the action) is, rather than at headquarters?

> *none*
> *at least a quarter*
> *at least half*
> *all*

SENSE OF MISSION

14a   Does the company have a statement of mission?

b   If asked to explain what the company mission was, would top management ...?

> *give an immediate, concise explanation*
> *wax eloquent for an hour or more*
> *waffle around the subject*
> *not understand the question*

15   What proportion of junior managers do you think would be able to describe the corporate mission accurately?

> *all*
> *more than half*
> *less than half*
> *none*

16   How strongly do you think top management really believes in the corporate mission?

> *totally*
> *fairly strongly*
> *difficult to say*
> *hardly at all*

17   What is top management's primary timeframe?

> *five years or more*
> *three to five years*
> *one to three years*
> *less than one year*

CLEAR OBJECTIVES DOWN THE LINE

18a   What proportion of employees do you believe fully understand what their objectives are?

> *all*
> *all managerial and professional staff*

most managerial and professional staff
key staff only

b Can all or most of them set those objectives in the context of the overall corporate plan?

19 When top management and the trade union representatives talk about the company's mission, does each of them understand what the other side is saying?

20 How often has substantial wastage occurred because people in the firm were beavering away on something that wasn't wanted?

never
rarely
often
it probably happens a lot but we don't know how to find out

THE PRACTICE OF LEADERSHIP

21 Do middle and junior managers regard the chief executive as an example they consciously wish to follow?

22 Do you have an effective system to reward good leadership?

23 How often does the word 'leadership' occur in your training manuals?

very frequently
occasionally
rarely
never

24a Does your company have a clear definition of what it means by leadership and of the kind of leaders it wants?

b Has it communicated that definition to all levels of management and supervision?

25 Do newly appointed managers automatically receive some form of leadership training?

26 Does the company measure leadership skills at various stages in people's careers?

27 Does the company know which positions are most critical in terms of needing high calibre leaders rather than managers?

28 Does your company provide frequent opportunity for people to practise leadership at a junior level?

29 Is the development of tomorrow's leaders part of the role of every line manager?

POINTS TO WATCH:

Question **5**: both leaders and managers are essential in today's corporate environment; ideally, a company should develop people with both abilities

Question **12**: if you answered every day or every week, then your chief executive probably isn't doing his job; he's doing yours

---

GENERAL POINTS

What the chief executive can do   Without doubt the key to developing a 'leadership culture' – a general perception in the organization that leaders are valued and encouraged – is the example of the chief executive and his top management team. Unless the chief executive can by his own attitude and behaviour demonstrate effective leadership, it will be difficult to find leadership below.

The chief executive must create an atmosphere in which the company believes in and values leadership. A good starting point is to establish how people feel about the leadership they are receiving. If employees feel that the people in charge of their destiny are indecisive, lacking direction and generally clueless, it is hardly likely that they will respond with the kind of commitment to the organization that characterizes companies with the winning streak. One of the problems in a great many executive suites is that top management never sees itself through the eyes of junior management or the shopfloor. The problem is not necessarily that middle and senior management is sycophantic (though that may indeed be the case), but rather that top management is unaware of how the image it presents to lower levels affects their motivation, and makes no attempt to identify how positive or negative that image is.

No matter how brilliant a manager you may be, you are only filling half the role of the chief executive if you cannot also be a good leader. You must ensure not only that you understand the difference between management and leadership, but that the key managers who report to you also share that understanding. It is a failing of the business schools that they churn out MBAs replete with analytical and problem-solving skills, but cannot teach them how to lead. That is one of the reasons why increasing attention is being paid to alternative schemes of management education stressing 'action learning'.

One of the problems of working from an ivory tower is that you have to make quite a lot of noise to capture the troops' attention. Most of what you do will never be observed outside the headquarters' inner circle. Part of leadership at this level is to be larger than life, so that people can see what you are doing without the need for binoculars. You don't, of course, have to indulge in dramatics, although it is remarkable how effective the 'Once more unto the breach' gambit can be in a crisis. You do have to make sure that the physical and hierarchical barriers that arise automatically in any large organization do not become stone walls. Your leadership will never be recognized if it is hidden away.

You can establish in various ways how the leadership qualities you and your top management colleagues present are evaluated. Don't dismiss what the stockbrokers' and Press reports say, just because you do not feel it is true. These sources have as much impact upon the attitudes and motivation of employees as they do upon share prices. Call the Press and the City in for informal discussions and ask them both for a frank opinion and the reasons they have formed that opinion; or have them surveyed by a professional research agency, which is more likely to extract the brutal criticisms that people are too polite to make to your face. You might also carry out attitude surveys of employees to determine their opinions.

If you have the courage to face this test, do not expect the replies to be comforting. You may well find key top management figures described as 'gutless' or 'unable to make a decision', and your whole top management team perceived as extras from *Dallas*. For leadership purposes this image, no matter how erroneous it may be, is the organizational reality, and it will change only if you make it change.

If the general image is not positive, if a significant proportion of people feel that you do not know what you are doing, there are only two likely explanations. One is that they are right, in which case you have some hard personal decision making to do. The other is that you are not projecting your aims, intentions and actions sufficiently well. Either way, it is a failure of leadership. In the following pages we will attempt to identify ways in which you can improve both your own leadership and that of the managers at all other levels in the organization.

What the individual manager can do   While the leadership style at the top may exert considerable restraints on how people below manage, you are still in many ways chief executive of your small part of the whole. As such, you too need to develop a leadership culture in your own subordinates – if only to ensure that there is someone ready to step into your shoes when a suitable promotion opportunity comes up.

Ask yourself: 'Am I predominantly a manager or a leader?' 'When I want people in my department to do something different, do they respond quickly and willingly, or is it always an uphill battle?' 'How do they regard me as a leader?' We all like to think we are 'natural' leaders, but in reality, for most of us, leadership is a skill that has to be learnt. You can begin to upgrade your leadership skills by recognizing the weaknesses in your leadership style. Try to attend a basic leadership course; read books on the subject; choose a few people in the organization who are manifestly good leaders and try to model your behaviour on theirs. Choose also a handful of bad leaders and identify what it is about their behaviour and attitudes that is so different from that of the good leaders. Then look closely at yourself again, to make sure you are not guilty of the same behaviour.

In sum, 'know thyself'. Remember, good leaders are in remarkably short supply in most organizations. If you can demonstrate leadership skills, your chances of entering and staying on the fast track are considerably improved.

Good leadership at lower levels in the organization does have at least one practical difference from leadership at the top. The distance – both physical and hierarchical – between you and your lowest-level subordinates is relatively small. So you do not need to present a larger-than-life image. Indeed it could, and probably would, be taken as mere posturing. You may well be far more effective (as will the chief executive in the sanctum of his own top management team) acting as the unobtrusive leader who makes things happen. The high personal profile is for effect outside the immediate team, not within it.

VISIBLE TOP MANAGEMENT

What the chief executive can do   It is easier to say 'Be visible' than to do it. The paperwork, telephone calls and meetings with outsiders still have to be attended to. But if managers in the most successful companies can, so can you. Sharing problems with people in the field is a remarkably effective way of gaining a new perspective on them, even if those employees lack understanding of the background. A company with 1000 employees has 1000 brains to think about every problem and every opportunity, if it can only learn how to harness them.

Simple but effective suggestions that apply to any corporate leader include the following:

- senior management should write into diaries at least two informal meetings a month with employees outside their normal circle. Some chief executives swear by breakfast or lunchtime meetings, where randomly selected employees from the same or different levels have the chance of face-to-face discussions on issues of concern to them. Most companies that have tried this approach report that people rarely use the opportunity for personal beefs; instead they focus closely on issues relating to the health of the company, or on general employee problems. Very often they bring up ideas they have been trying to pass on for ages, or have not known whom to tell about. Many of these ideas may have practical application.
- hold meetings in the operating unit rather than the headquarters building, whenever possible. Not only will top management learn more, but you will have the opportunity to speak to far more people.
- when holding meetings with groups of employees, stop first and consider *why* you are doing so. Too often executives see these

occasions as mere internal public relations, a necessary exercise in providing enough information to prevent industrial unrest. They provide facts, or at least as many as they consider essential, but little else. Yet these meetings are an opportunity to do much more. They can be used to show that you care about the company, and about the people who work in it. They can be used to explain your thinking – why you took particular decisions. And most of all they can be an opportunity to *listen.*

- don't let the niceties of hierarchical responsibilities prevent you from going directly to lower-level employees for information. At the very least your call will convince the subordinate you are still alive and kicking. (It is remarkable how many employees perceive the group chief executive as a kind of Howard Hughes, presumed alive only because no one has seen the body.) At best, it is an excellent opportunity to motivate a junior employee. Try calling people up to congratulate them on a task particularly well done, then follow it up with a note. You may be surprised how much you learn in the process.

- use the full range of communications available to get your message across to employees: what is important to you, where the company is going, what problems you are tackling and what opportunities you are trying to seize

- examine the impression you make on employees. You may not be able to change your nature; indeed, you may well look ridiculous if you try. One chief executive who was advised by a consultant to smile more, was immediately assumed by his subordinates to have gone mad when he tried to put the advice into practice. It was simply too radically different from the normal image they had of him. What all corporate leaders *can* do is start with the more obvious signals. If you roll up at 10 am and leave at 3 pm every day, you can hardly expect to motivate other employees to work long hours. Similarly, buying an expensive new car or indulging in costly executive suite refurbishment while trying to implement an austerity programme (both examples encountered in different companies within the same week) is unlikely to guarantee success. By the same token, visible gestures such as arriving before other staff and suffering austerity along with the rest can be strong reinforcements to a positive image of top management as hard-working and caring. But don't overdo it. Exchanging the Rolls for a Metro may well be misinterpreted as a sign of desperation (one chairman of a now-defunct company did just that, although he kept the chauffeur). Neither is it necessary for you to do everyone else's job for them; that simply negates any expression of confidence in their abilities.

● be as honest with yourself as you possibly can when you ask 'How do I want to be regarded?' and 'How well do my behaviour and attitudes actually fit that image?' The analysis of employees' opinions and attitudes can be a useful measure, and should not be dismissed as 'ill-informed'. The degree to which the employees truly are 'ill-informed' about their leaders, especially at top management level, is a measure of top management's success or failure in achieving constructive visibility. It is, of course, much easier to correct wrong perceptions than to convince people that the correct perceptions they have are, in fact, wrong. So, if members of the top management team cannot summon up real personal involvement and commitment to the company, if they cannot share the sense of mission, or if they lack the ability to inspire others with the mission, then the chief executive must consider either replacing them or moving them aside into a position where they can do no harm. Those executives who do have these qualities will not find it difficult to demonstrate them, given the time and the opportunity.

● examine the amount of time you devote each month to activities that make you visible. If it is less than 20 per cent, you should seriously re-examine your calendar.

What the individual manager can do   You don't have to be a chief executive to put these lessons into effect. Learning them is a matter of practice, and the best time to practise is as a junior manager or supervisor. Skills learned at an early stage in a business career tend to stick.

Whether you are the chief executive or the most junior supervisor, you can lead by telling people below you what you have done and why it is important, and putting their part into context. The guidelines on leadership issued by The Industrial Society include the advice: 'Regularly walk round each person's place of work; observe, listen and praise.' Peters and Waterman refer to this as 'Management by Walking About' (MBWA).

When Sweden first experimented with semi-autonomous work groups, one of the principal causes of failure was that the shopfloor employees felt isolated from their supervisors. The work groups had taken over so many of the supervisor's routine organizing and checking tasks that he spent most of his day handling paperwork in an office. The Swedish employers learnt to put the supervisor back on to the shop floor where he was able to offer advice and guidance and to give the employees confidence that someone was concerned about their problems. Good leadership demands a regular and frequent physical presence.

SENSE OF MISSION

What the chief executive can do   There is a great deal of difference between a strategic plan and a corporate mission. The former is limited in time and scope; it may change radically from one year to the next and is rarely the same five years later. The corporate mission, on the other hand, is a long-term, far more slowly evolving set of objectives that permeate the organization, giving it both stability and direction. It is, perhaps, a reason for being. 'Why are we here?' may sound a rather philosophical question. But it is in reality a most practical starting point for determining where the organization should be going. Unless the top management team has a clear and shared concept of why the company is in business, the chances of getting everyone pulling in the same direction are not high.

The company without any sense of mission at the top probably does not have an effective leader and its problems will only be resolved by a new chief executive. Even the most detailed strategic plans are of little value if they are not set in the larger context of a corporate mission. The mission provides the stability and continuity within which successive strategic planning cycles can operate. It focuses top management's minds on a timeframe well beyond the normal planning horizon and, in many cases, beyond their own retirement dates.

Not everyone is a visionary. But most management teams can develop a vision. The starting point is where the organization should ideally be. There will undoubtedly be differing views among the top management team. But hammering those differences out is a critical part of creating the corporate sense of mission. It is also important that top management should aim to reach a consensus based not on the lowest common denominators, but upon the highest aspirations of those in the organization. Those aspirations will usually be based on a few fundamental 'core values', some of which may already be part of the organization's culture.

Ordinary employees often have as good a feel as management, or better, for the core values of an organization. One large company we have encountered has undergone so many radical organizational changes and staff movements that top management assumed that any core values or integral corporate culture had been lost for good. It emerged, however, that only senior management had abandoned the core values completely; that the employees themselves would respond well to a high service ethic, if only permitted and encouraged to do so. Rather than create a whole new corporate mission, all that was needed was to resurrect an old one. The moral: good values die hard.

This same company had concocted as its statement of mission that it wanted to be the best in its industry. Not only was this a somewhat mediocre ambition – the best being still unacceptably poor – but the statement did not define what it meant by being best, nor what had to be done to achieve that modest ambition. High-flown sentiments are of little value on their own. The essence of the corporate mission is that it ties philosophy and the long-term vision to a practical road map of where the company is going.

There is also a need to be adventurous in formulating the corporate mission. This is no occasion to be timid. Set your sights high, then start planning to hit the target. Don't worry if the vision sounds impossibly grandiose. There are only three criteria by which it should be judged. Those are:

- does it oblige the organization to strive for something far beyond its current achievements?
- do you and your top management team believe it is both desirable and humanly achievable?
- are you truly committed to it?

Only if you can answer yes to all three will you establish a true sense of corporate mission.

Having created a sense of corporate mission at the highest levels, you now need to communicate it to employees, suppliers and customers. The most effective way to spread your commitment and beliefs is the way the faithful have done for thousands of years. Preach to all who will listen. You have one advantage over the missionary who, in modern times at least, does not have a captive audience. In a corporation, employees *have* to listen to their managers – their jobs depend on doing so. The more strongly you believe in the corporate mission, the easier it will be to convince others. At the same time, you can reinforce the message in two ways:

● with a written statement of mission
● by controlling what actually happens in the organization

The written statement of mission need not be long. But it must be more than just pious phrases and hopes. It must be a clear philosophy, backed up with examples wherever possible. It should include qualitative as well as quantitative objectives. People react better to quantitative objectives in the short term; qualitative in the long term.

Everything that happens in the company either reinforces or weakens the corporate mission. Top management needs to examine, among other things:

● the reward system: whether a correct interpretation of the corporate mission leads to reward rather than penalty
● the promotion system: what sort of people actually get promoted? How well do they fit the profile of an ideal manager as inferred from the statement of mission?
● output from the organization: if the corporate mission emphasizes quality of service, for example, do the departments concerned take it seriously?

Action – sometimes radical – then needs to be taken to ensure that what happens is as close as possible to what the company aspires to in the statement of mission. Once again, your example, the commitment you demonstrate towards the various elements of the statement of mission, will be of substantial influence in how easily that gap between objective and reality is filled.

What the individual manager can do   You cannot create a sense of mission for the company as a whole. But you can outline what you consider the core values of your own department to be. Most people like to work within an understandable framework of basic principles, inside which they can make their own choices, judgements and decisions. Very few managers ever lay their principles out to new recruits. It is not that they have no principles; merely that they have never undertaken the discipline of putting them into a coherent, rational form. The benefits of doing so are more than simply telling people what they can and can't do. The basic principles help your subordinates to think as you do, making it easier for you to delegate. Moreover, you may find them of value when you have a difficult decision to make, because they form a ready yardstick, solidly based in your own experience.

CLEAR OBJECTIVES DOWN THE LINE

What the chief executive can do   It is the statement of mission that makes clear objectives possible. It provides a broad framework within which the individual's objectives in the organization make sense. The objectives will make even more sense if they are expressed in terms of key tasks (together with a description of why those tasks are important to the overall corporate objectives) rather than broken down into a detailed list of instructions such as so many companies attempt to enforce. This is particularly true at the lowest levels in the organization, where many companies find setting objectives so difficult that they do not bother. Yet even if they are not tied into an incentive or performance appraisal scheme, these people are capable of working to broad objectives. They can, for example, agree with their supervisor what has to be achieved in a given period, the resources available for the task and why the task is important to the company.

Your company probably has a 'cascading' scheme of management by objectives, in which objectives filter down from level to level. If that scheme is like most others, it will suffer from the problem of 'Chinese whispers'. Each layer in the hierarchy distorts the objectives of people below to cater for some whim or side objective of its own. The result is that few people at the bottom ever have anything like the objectives that top management would have intended. Tasks that should get done fall by the wayside, while people waste time on activities that should never have been started.

You can avoid that dispersion of effort and energy by making sure that everyone understands the broad context in which their objectives have been set. This requires a degree of openness about plans and strategies that many companies will find alien. It means that each layer in the organization must not only receive a much fuller picture of what top management is aiming for, but must be persuaded to pass on the bulk of that information to the next layer down.

It also means that the trade union side, if there is one, must be given far greater access to the planning process, so that it can reinforce the message in its own discussions with employees. If the union presents to them a different interpretation of top management's intentions and motivations to that coming down through the management hierarchy, confusion, distrust and a greatly reduced level of commitment and compliance can be expected on the shopfloor. If, on the other hand, the message from both sources is the same, then most people will accept what they are told.

The union representatives can, of course, only play this co-operative role if they understand exactly what your vision of the future is. You have to spend time with them explaining and discussing the long-term mission of the company and how it might be fulfilled. They probably won't agree with everything you say, nor is it essential that they should so so. What is vital is that they should be convinced that you are genuinely committed to the corporate mission and the immediate objectives resulting from it. Only then can you be reasonably sure that the right message about objectives is permeating the organization.

What the individual manager can do A significant part of the leadership role at any level involves discussing objectives with subordinates, ensuring that everyone knows what he is to do, why he should do it and how it fits into the overall scheme of things. This is not a task to perform at formal six-monthly or annual assessments. It must be a day-to-day activity, part of the normal round of discussion and exchange of information. The effective leader constantly talks over objectives and in doing so not only reinforces subordinates' understanding of them, but learns quickly of problems likely to arise. The frequent discussion also means, of course, that objectives can be altered swiftly and relatively painlessly, with everyone concerned aware of what is happening and why. This kind of flexibility, which depends heavily on how confident everyone feels regarding the relationship of their task to the corporate mission as well as to short-term objectives, is not particularly common in British or European companies.

THE PRACTICE OF LEADERSHIP

What the chief executive can do   The example set by top management has enormous impact on the style and quality of leadership at
other levels in the organization. High visibility helps – at least when
the senior managers are able to project a desirable image – but is
only a partial answer. Top management has to go out of its way to
demonstrate what it values in terms of leadership. That requires a
commitment of time to activities which, on the surface, may appear
trivial and irrelevant.

For example, if one of the firm's delivery drivers is injured in a
road accident while at work, a personal note from top management
will be remembered long after he has recovered. Similarly, personal
intervention by the chairman on apparently minor matters, such as
the quality of packaging or how an individual customer was dealt
with, tends to reinforce the employees' perceptions of what is regarded as important within the company. Such interventions swiftly
become part of the corporate folklore.

In talking to managers, top management should take every opportunity to stress why leadership is important to the company and
what leadership qualities are particularly looked for. It can draw
upon the company folklore for examples.

Other methods of reinforcing the leadership message are:

- hammer home the leadership message in every available form of
  internal company communication, from the personnel handbook
  to the employee newspaper. Make sure everyone in the company
  understands what you mean by good leadership.
- reward good leadership through prize schemes, general recognition and salary increments
- ensure that developing leadership skills is a line, rather than a
  staff, responsibility and that all managers are evaluated on their
  success in helping subordinates learn how to lead
- build leadership training into the development programme, at
  least for all employees with supervisory or managerial potential.
  Deliberately place them in an environment where they *have* to
  exert leadership early in their career. Even very green employees
  can often take on a project of their own. Don't be afraid to set
  a challenge: the future leaders the company needs will not be

daunted. Indeed, they are likely to relish it. One of the principal reasons for high turnover among young management level recruits in many organizations is the *lack* of challenge while they are learning the ropes. The more challenge the company can provide, the more these key people will relish their jobs. There is also some evidence that the earlier people acquire leadership skills, the more effective managers they will be.

● identify those managerial positions where leadership qualities are particularly important. Make it clear to everyone that the successful candidate was selected because of his leadership qualities, and be prepared to pay over the odds for the right person.

What the individual manager can do   Middle and junior managers can establish the same folklore in their own departments. You can also look for ways in which to develop your own leadership skills. Among things you can do are:

● actively seek opportunities to exert leadership. Volunteer for some of those hot potatoes no one else will handle, such as the loss-making subsidiary or the department with a terrible industrial relations record. Here you should normally be able to write your own ticket in terms of the freedom you have to run things your own way. When things are that desperate, any determined manager can make some improvements through good leadership. You are also likely to obtain the support of the people within the unit, because they are almost certainly longing for someone to lead them out of the mess they are in. It will do wonders for your image – and that, in turn, is likely to be valuable to your career prospects.

● ask for feedback from more senior management: 'Could I have handled that better?' They will be pleased to tell you, and discussion of your leadership style will be handled in an atmosphere of positive analysis rather than of negative criticism.

● look at the style and degree of leadership needed in the senior or middle management position you aspire to. Can you duplicate that now? If not, what experience do you need to grow that ability? If you can, persuade a senior manager to act as mentor, providing you with the leadership learning experiences you need.

● if the leadership experience you need is not readily available inside the company, look outside. Can you obtain it through spare-time work with a voluntary organization or a professional body?

● above all, prepare for yourself a self-development programme in which leadership qualities are important. Through discussion, reading and observation, establish what those qualities are and assess how far you have to go to be in full possession of them. Guru of leadership John Adair expresses the point succinctly in his book *Effective Leadership*: 'the best way to learn leadership is to do your present job as well as possible. ... If you can develop the insight to monitor your leadership performance, then even mistakes and failures will disclose positive lessons.'

2 Winning through autonomy

Somewhere in the spectrum between total bureaucratic inflexibility and institutional anarchy lies the ideal blend of control and autonomy for each company. That blend may not be constant. Like the ribbon in the middle of the tug-of-war rope, it moves to and fro according to the strength of competing influences.

The level of autonomy and control may vary considerably even inside the same organization. The character and style of divisional heads in a decentralized holding company may create a wide variation in the amount of autonomy permitted to middle and junior managers. The kind of business may also have a significant effect. For example, businesses where standardized customer service is essential may have less room for independent action, while high-tech development may only work in an environment where new ideas can be tried out with the minimum of bureaucracy.

So, when the right level of autonomy is a variable quantity, how do you tell whether your organization gives people the freedom they need to do their job most effectively? Some of the questions you might ask in a large company include:

GENERAL QUESTIONS

1 Which of the following statements best describes your company?

> *top management is afraid of losing control; it is constantly looking over people's shoulders*
>
> *top management believes in substantial autonomy within a clear and unobtrusive framework of simple controls*
>
> *top management believes that the only way to get the best out of people is to give them complete autonomy; if they want help they'll call for it*

2   What is your company's attitude to the idea of limited numbers of managerial and professional employees working some or most of the time from home, linked to their office by computer?

> *positive: it has already carried out a number of successful experiments*
> *cautious: it foresees a lot of practical problems*
> *totally opposed: how would it know what they were doing?*

SMALL HEADQUARTERS BUREAUCRACIES

3   How big is your group headquarters?

> *just a handful of people*
> *100 or so*
> *100 to 500*
> *more than 500*

4   Where are most of the major operating decisions taken, e.g. investment in a particularly expensive piece of equipment?

> *in the field*
> *at HQ*

5   How does the foyer compare with the backroom offices or shop-floor?

> *we spend more on the back offices – our people deserve comfort*
> *we think it's more important to have an impressive foyer than comfortable offices*

6   Compare the annual running costs and the asset value of the headquarters building with those of the production units. Which of the following statements is nearest the truth?

> *running costs and/or asset value of even fairly small production units are significantly higher than those of the HQ*
> *running costs and/or asset value of fairly small production units are about the same as those of the HQ*
> *running costs and/or asset value of HQ and average production unit are about the same*

*running costs and/or asset value of HQ are higher than those of
an average production unit*
*running costs and/or asset value of HQ are very much higher than
those of an average production unit*

7   How many levels are there between (group) top management and
the first level of supervision?

three or less
four to seven
more than seven

8a   Where do young managers see the greatest promotion prospects?

in the field
at headquarters

b   And where are the most talented junior and middle managers
in the company concentrated?

in the field
at headquarters

SMALL, INDEPENDENT BUSINESS UNITS

9   What is the average size of major operating units in your company?

Less than 500 people
500 to 1000 people
more than 1000 people

10   How frequently does the unit head have to refer upwards for
approval?

never
a few times a year
monthly
weekly
daily

11   How much on-the-spot decision-making authority do your company's people in the field have compared with the competition?

> *far more*
> *some more*
> *about the same*
> *a bit less*
> *a lot less*

12   For which of the following functions does total or near-total responsibility (within an agreed budget) rest with the operating unit?

> *marketing*
> *production*
> *sales and distribution*
> *capital investment*
> *industrial relations/personnel*

13   How close to being an entrepreneurial organization is your company?

> *totally*
> *quite*
> *not very*
> *quite the opposite; this is a pure bureaucracy*

14   Has your company set up any semi-autonomous subsidiaries, where entrepreneurs (from inside or outside) retain a significant share in the business?

> *yes*
> *no, but intend to*
> *no, but thinking about it*
> *no, not likely to*
> *no, totally opposed*

15   How do unit managers perceive corporate headquarters?

> *as a lifeline when things go wrong*
> *as a cost centre*
> *as a bank*
> *as a priesthood*
> *as an ivory tower*

16   Does the general climate within the company encourage entrepreneurial behaviour?

INFORMAL SYSTEMS OF WORKING TOGETHER

17   Are conflicts of interest between different operating units usually resolved ... ?

> *swiftly by discussion*
> *slowly by discussion*
> *allowed to fester till top management has to intervene*

18   How long does it normally take between requests from operating units and decisions by top management?

> *a matter of days at most*
> *up to a week*
> *up to a month*
> *over a month*

19   Take the basic tasks of your industry (e.g. in publishing, bringing a book from manuscript to publication; in manufacturing, bringing a new product on stream). Does your company do this in ...?

> *a significantly shorter time than its competitors*
> *about the same time as its competitors*
> *significantly longer time than its competitors*

20a   Does the culture of the organization as a whole make it easy for *ad hoc* teams to form to tackle problems and opportunities?

b   Do these teams automatically assume a degree of authority?

21   How much notice is taken of the recommendations of such teams?

> *they are there to make decisions*
> *top management usually acts on their recommendations*
> *top management occasionally acts on their recommendations*
> *it's just a talking shop; the ideas are rarely implemented*

22 How often does top management give direct orders?

> *hardly ever*
> *sometimes*
> *frequently*

DELEGATION DOWN THE LINE

23 If asked whether they were allowed to use their initiative sufficiently what would most junior/middle managers reply?

> *yes*
> *sometimes*
> *not often*
> *never*
> *no one would ask such a question*

24 Do managers in your company feel that being seen to delegate more and more of their job ...?

> *improves their chances of promotion and new responsibilities*
> *increases their chances of being made redundant*

25 How many middle managers does your company have, compared to junior managers?

> *one middle manager for twenty or more junior managers*
> *one middle manager for ten to twenty junior managers*
> *one middle manager for less than ten junior managers*

A POSITIVE ATTITUDE TOWARDS RISK TAKING

26 Is the differential in rewards for taking 'high-risk' managerial jobs (compared to the normal 'safe' job in a successful operation) ...?

> *very high if you perform*
> *high*
> *moderate or no differential*
> *lower than in successful operations*

27   What happens to managers whose projects fail?

> *they are encouraged to try again with a better product*
> *they are encouraged to try again but given a black mark*
> *they are shunted aside or demoted*
> *they are fired*

28   Does your company reduce the risks in new ventures ...?

> *by pursuing only ventures that appear to be profitable even with a*
> *very large margin of error*
> *by pouring money and effort into detailed planning, preparation*
> *and market research*
> *by not pursuing new ventures at all*

29   How easy is it for a manager with a good idea, and a detailed case, to obtain unbudgeted finance to pursue it?

> *straightforward*
> *complex*
> *virtually impossible*

30   Do people in your company feel free to admit mistakes?

> *yes, it's expected*
> *no, you're asking for trouble*

31   There often seems to be a correlation between the size of risks taken and the size of a person's or company's ambition. In the past five years has your company taken ...?

> *numerous large investment risks*
> *a few large investment risks*
> *no large investment risks*

GENERALIST MANAGERS

32   Does your company expose specialist managers to general management experience ...?

> *at age twenty-five to thirty*
> *at age thirty-one to forty*
> *at age forty-one plus*

33 If you as manager of your operating unit were able to buy it out of the company tomorrow, would you make . . .?

> *very few changes – I'm already running it/I can run it in the way I think best*
> *moderate changes – we'd throw out some of the reporting systems*
> *major changes – I know how to run this operation most profitably, but top management won't let me*

POINTS TO WATCH:

Question 1: autonomy without controls is abdication. Companies with the winning streak combine autonomy with simple controls.

Question 5: companies with the winning streak don't go overboard on either. The golden rule in both cases is to be smart but functional.

Question 15: the only healthy attitude among all the alternative answers is as a bank (see later in this chapter for the explanation)

Question 28: it is the second alternative that characterizes winning streak companies. Anything that seems so risk-free that it can't fail usually has a very serious catch, even if you can't see it now. Hence the importance of market research.

GENERAL POINTS

What the chief executive can do If your organization is more centralized and bureaucratic than is healthy if it is to become a winner, it is only one of very many. The need to control operations from one place was born at a time when both management methods and communications technology were far less effective than they are now. The Victorian manager insisted upon having people where he could see them because he had no other way of ensuring that he was getting value for money from their work. It was a case of 'out of sight, out of control'. That is no longer true. The new communications technologies, which make it possible for a whole range of specialist and clerical staff to work from their own living rooms, make large headquarters functionally obsolete, if they were not already socially so. In today's business world, let alone tomorrow's, the centralized bureaucracy is a dinosaur – be it a ravaging *Tyrannosaurus rex* or a somnolent *Diplodocus*.

You can start to unravel the bureaucracy of your organization by looking first at the attitudes of your senior and top management colleagues. The desire for excessive control arises usually out of fear, particularly through executives' lack of confidence either in their own ability to handle the complexities of managing the modern corporation or in that of middle and junior management to avoid costly mistakes. Changing that attitude is rather like prising a rifle from the hands of a shell-shocked soldier – you have to pull open one finger at a time to release his frozen grip.

To manage uncertainty, flexibility and autonomy are essential. The executive who cannot cope with the different style of management required in a network of semi-autonomous units is, to put it bluntly, obsolete in the modern corporation. Look at each of your executive colleagues and ask the following questions:

● how much time do they spend thinking about the business and how much time on operational matters? People unable to relax direct controls rarely have time to concentrate their efforts on strategy.

● what record do they have of developing others to take tasks over from them? Excessively control-oriented managers are rarely good mentors. Their organization is frequently weakened by lack of replacement talent.

● how many major issues can they deal with at one time? Managing the decentralized organization requires considerable mental flexibility.

Some of these excessively control-oriented attitudes and behaviour may be caused by structures of the organization rather than by the personality of the individual executives. You will never really know until you change the organization and can observe how they perform in a different environment.

Changing the organization's structure is worth a book on its own, and indeed there are dozens of books on the subject. An understanding of how organizations develop is a useful, if not essential, foundation to the changes you need to initiate; that is a topic we cover in the appendix to this book. Whatever the stage of your company's development you should be able to set ambitious targets for reorganizing it along entrepreneurial lines. In particular you will want to maximize flexibility where it matters, while preventing independent action from going to extremes. One useful guideline to use for any structure you design is 'Does it help or hinder teamwork?' Effective autonomy, in the business sense, gives a unit head the freedom to do things in his own way and the responsibility to make sure that in doing so, he is working with rather than against the rest of the company.

What the individual manager can do   Could your unit operate more autonomously? If you think it could, draw up and present to your immediate superior a plan of the changes that could be made and what benefits they would bring. In particular, stress how they would help him, by freeing his time for more useful activities. The plan may not be accepted, but you will at least have registered a claim for more responsibility. One possible result may be a transfer to an area where greater autonomy will be permitted. The earlier you learn to operate autonomously, the more likely you are to recognize and seize opportunities for advancement.

SMALL HEADQUARTERS BUREAUCRACIES

What the chief executive can do   You can tell a great deal about the attitudes of a company by comparing its headquarters building with its factories, or the foyer of its offices with the rooms where the staff work. Virtually every penny you spend on the headquarters is unproductive, because it contributes neither to sales nor production. If you could cut your headquarters operating costs in half, what could you do with the cash in the field? Could you, for example, re-equip with more modern facilities an old plant coming under threat from competitors? The comparison between what that money is doing now and what it could be doing should be enough to make any chief executive undertake regular reviews of spending on headquarters buildings.

Several years ago, a large US multinational company simultaneously made a number of its field sales force redundant and redecorated the office of the new expatriate chief executive of its British operations. The veneered panelling and imported Swedish furniture that went into the office outweighed the entire annual savings from the staff reduction. The chief's explanation that the money came from a different budget and that he needed a prestigious office to impress customers failed to cut much ice with the employees. Nor with the customer who, when invited to admire the décor, commented that the money might better have been spent hiring a better grade of typist, who could spell his company's name correctly.

Such gauche behaviour may be an extreme, but it does illustrate the principle that both customers and employees prefer to see money being spent on improving the company and its products than on inessential frills. Of course, there is a minimum level of smartness and presentation that any company with winning ambitions must have, to avoid appearing slapdash and scruffy. You certainly don't want to give customers the impression that you are so cash-starved you can't afford a properly equipped reception area, for example. One way of creating the right balance is to look at your foyer or your headquarters building and ask:

- does it produce anything we can sell?
- does it sell anything we produce?
- would the absence of all or part of it harm our efforts to produce or sell?

If the answer to all three is 'no', either you don't need it, or you could make do with something much less extensive and expensive, or you should be looking closely at its function to determine if it *could* fulfil the three criteria above. Some companies, for example, have turned their foyers into exhibition and customer reception areas, where every inch is devoted to selling.

There is enough experience now among companies, which have slimmed down in the late 1970s and early 1980s, to show that cutting headquarters numbers, while never painless, does not normally cause any permanent damage to the organization. Indeed, the evidence suggests that the removal of middle management layers facilitates communications. Deprived of genuine control functions in an era where decisions have to be made swiftly, middle management in many companies has perforce become a filter between top management and the ground floor where the action is. Not only does much middle management slow communications and decision making, but it may filter out the very information top management needs. Some chief executives who have sliced whole layers from their organization charts have been stirred to do so by the frequency with which they have had to bypass middle management to find out what is going on in the field.

Looking at the problem the other way round, the more layers of management you have, the more you need a large headquarters to hold them and their secretarial assistants. You certainly don't want them tripping over each other in the operational units, getting in the way of the people who actually do the work. Indeed, if you wish to be cynical, you can look upon the large headquarters as an asylum used, if not intended, to keep middle management out of harm's way.

So what needs to be done? The first step is to ask two simple questions: 'What functions could be transferred to the field?' and 'What functions absolutely have to be at headquarters?' The answer to the first question is usually 'Practically all'; to the second, 'Very few'. A handful of key directors may need to be at the centre of decision making. But putting their decisions into practice is a task undertaken far more effectively on site, in the operating units, by people who are closely in touch with what is happening in that unit and in its market. The only tasks that should be retained at headquarters are those which cannot efficiently be assigned to an operating unit.

An important aspect of breaking up the concentration of power in the centre of the organization is the attitude of talented junior and middle managers to where the best promotion prospects lie. As long as career fast tracks are concentrated in the centre, every manager worth his salt will be spending half his time scheming how to get there or how to avoid being sent back out to the field. You have to change that attitude by changing the rules. Insist that, under normal circumstances, promotion to certain levels can only take place after experience as department head in an operating unit or as head of a field sales branch. Publicly identify a handful of high flyers and appoint them to senior jobs in the regions. Compare the compensation package of people at headquarters and in the field and adjust it to give an edge to the person in the field. As one chief executive, who had done just that, told us, 'The key people I want to appoint to headquarters jobs are all refusing to leave the field, because they are earning such high bonuses. It means we have to make some more adjustments to the compensation scheme, but I'm delighted.'

What the individual manager can do Top management holds all the cards in this hand. But it may well pay you to keep looking over their shoulders, waiting for them to shuffle the pack. Are you, for

example, in one of the layers of management or in a headquarters
department likely to go? Make yourself a safety net by the following
actions, among others:

● make sure your desire to act more autonomously is recognized
by those above
● initiate or become involved with strategic projects for an operating unit likely to survive any purge. Establish a natural position
there to move into, should top management decide to break up
your headquarters department and move it into the field.
● 'draw up your own proposals for dispersing your department
among the operating units. Hang on to it until you hear the first
rumours of change. Then send it to both your immediate superior
and the chief executive.

SMALL, INDEPENDENT BUSINESS UNITS

What the chief executive can do   When Fritz Schumacher wrote
'small is beautiful' he was spitting into the wind. Now the wind has
turned and even many of the largest companies are scurrying to turn
themselves into confederations of small business units.

You can take a number of immediate steps to make that happen
in your company. Firstly, you can issue policy guidelines setting a
maximum size for any operation within the group. You will have to
decide what that figure should be in relation to your industry and its
historical legacy of plants and offices. For most companies the maximum rational size of a new facility seems to be between 200 and
500 people. Above that, the unit chief executive begins to lose contact
with both the people and the operations.

Fortunately, the whole direction of technology seems to be pushing
towards smaller, more capital-intensive production units. These units
usually produce as much as, if not more than, their predecessors, but
in less space, with fewer people. You can therefore normally afford to
be fairly rigorous as to the maximum number of people employed on
one site. Even on existing sites with several thousand people, it is
frequently possible to break operations up into independent units,
each with its own management structure and identifiable chief executive leader. Think of the arrangement as an industrial park. People
may pass through the same gate in the morning and evening, eat in

the same canteen and leave their car in the same car park; but they owe their loyalty to and receive recognition from their own small company, rather than from the large parent.

How much autonomy should these small business units have? As much as possible. Each should have responsibility for every aspect of its affairs, except those where a strong and valid argument can be made for retaining a centralized control. This is an issue we will cover in more depth in the next chapter, but here it suffices to say that the number of issues where such an argument can genuinely be made will normally be few. Once senior management of the unit has agreed with group top management its budget for the year, it should have near-total freedom to use the resources available to fulfil or exceed its targets as it sees fit. In particular, the small business unit must have the authority to respond rapidly to changes in its market, challenges from competitors and new technical developments. It has, in short, to be market-oriented – something a bureaucracy, almost by definition, can never be.

In practice, many companies find it difficult to make such a major transformation in one go. Hence the popularity of an alternative approach, which allows top management to get used to the feel of having entrepreneurs in the business without having them disrupting the company as a whole. Recognizing that the entrepreneur cannot function easily within the control systems of the traditional large company organization, some companies now put entrepreneurial individuals into special divisions not subject to the normal rules and controls of the rest of the company. While there must be *some* controls, these are deliberately maintained at the lowest level necessary to prevent major misuse of resources. Neither fully in nor fully outside the company, they are both cocooned from it and prevented from infecting it. Most British companies fight shy of giving equity to the managers who lead these ventures, although the practice is becoming common in the United States and has much to commend it. For one thing, the equity stake raises the entrepreneurial manager's level of commitment to the project. Some companies have gone so far as to retain only a minority stake, to encourage the seconded manager to take on the entrepreneurial role to the full.

If you can successfully break down the company into a network of autonomous business units you will find that attitudes towards what remains of headquarters will gradually change. From resenting it as an intrusive, overbearing presence, unit managers will gradually come to recognize it as a resource, providing advice and finance to enable them to carry out their entrepreneurial plans.

One important measure of the degree of real autonomy practised in a company is where the decisions are taken. We recommend that every company should carry out a periodic *decision audit*. The audit should cover a period of, say, two weeks chosen at random from the year, and detail every decision referred to headquarters by a field operation and every decision taken at headquarters but relating to an individual operating unit. Most of these decisions will be routine and can simply be recorded in terms of volume, rather than individually, so the effort required in gathering data need not be vast, especially if the exercise is confined to individual headquarters departments, rather than to HQ as a whole.

From the picture this information builds up may emerge a number of obvious anomalies, issues that are clearly far too trivial to be decided at headquarters. Other matters (for example, capital expenditure beyond the authority of the operating unit) are equally clearly the province of headquarters. In between, however, is likely to be a mass of greyer areas where it is necessary to ask:

● could this decision have been made equally well in the field?
● would the decision have been the same or different? And if different, would the decision in the field have been better, in terms of background knowledge and results?

Examining a small number of key decisions, chosen both from those made in the field and from those made at headquarters, immediately after the decision was taken and six months or a year later (when the results are beginning to show) can also be revealing. Certain types of decisions may show a distinctly better pattern of success in the field, for example. Analysing the patterns of decision making allows management to decide more precisely what needs to be decided at headquarters and what could as easily be left to people at the sharp end of the business.

What the individual manager can do If you haven't evaluated what you want out of your management career, now is the time to do so. If you want a safe, unexciting existence, where you are implementing rather than making decisions, then a bureaucratic environment is probably right for you. But don't expect it to be a secure billet, for the bureaucratic company that cannot change has a dubious future.

If, on the other hand, you are seeking challenge, excitement and responsibility you are most likely to find it in a decentralized, networked company that values autonomy and rewards initiative. That is not to say, however, that a centralized company cannot also provide some autonomy for those who look for it. The art is to determine what the rules do allow you to do, rather than concentrate on what they prevent you from doing. There is, for example, considerable scope for retail managers to influence what happens in their branch, simply by how well or badly they motivate their staff.

It would also be wrong to conclude that all standardized service businesses have to be tightly controlled from the centre. The service expected from the milk roundsman, for example, is the only selling point for home delivery. Yet the trend of the future is to allow the roundsmen to become independent franchisees. The paradox is that these 'independent' operators may in reality be both freer and more tightly controlled than before: running their own business obliges them to take note of costs and service to a degree that could not normally be expected when they were only employees. The threat of the loss of franchise may be more powerful than the threat of dismissal from employment.

Whatever the business you are in, there will be niches where some degree of autonomy of action is not only tolerated but encouraged. Talk to more senior managers about where those niches lie or how they could be created, and stake your claim.

INFORMAL SYSTEMS OF WORKING TOGETHER

What the chief executive can do   You are the final arbiter in any dispute between operating units. In theory, the more autonomy you grant to small business units, the greater the chances that two or more of them will pursue the same market, the same project or the same area of R&D. Part of your role as the network-maker is to forestall such conflicts by creating constructive dialogue between units and across divisions. The more formal you make the rules and regulations that govern interactions between units, the more you are likely to restrict their autonomy and creative energy. Rather, place an obligation on units to work out their problems together and insist that failure to agree will be seen as a failure of management on both sides. In this way, the units will spend less time defending their patch against other units inside the company and more working out how they can use their mutual energies to defend against attack from outside.

What the individual manager can do What applies to relations between unit heads applies to yours too. Good teamworkers are highly valued in all excellent companies. You can make your unit run more smoothly by working hard at building your team skills. The good teamworker not only works easily with other people, but helps them work with each other. He recognizes and reconciles different points of view, foresees and averts potential conflict, and attempts to make up for weaknesses within the team by drafting in additional help. By and large, he does this in an informal, unobtrusive manner; the more formal and obvious his efforts are, the more likely they are to be resisted.

You can learn these skills by observing how other good teamworkers behave and by asking for training in team working. Become familiar with the various techniques available, such as transactional analysis and neuro-linguistic programming and try them out to see which work for you.

DELEGATION DOWN THE LINE

What the chief executive can do The next step is to take a critical look at delegation within the company. How well do the company culture and the structure of the organization encourage or discourage delegation?

Some of the issues that need to be looked at are:

● how secure are people in the various management levels? The higher their anxiety level, the less willing in general they will be to delegate. Where anxiety levels are high, the chances are that top management has failed to get across its aims and objectives credibly: people either do not know what is going on and what the likely implications for them are, or they do not believe what they have been told. Paradoxically this anxiety can be high in a period of stability, as stories of impending storms circulate, and low in a period of great change. The difference lies in how well the top management has sold its message, how well it has convinced other employees that it really knows what it is doing and has their welfare at heart.

● does the organization structure encourage delegation? The more levels in the corporate hierarchy, the less manoeuvrability there is for people to relinquish part of their jobs. Conversely, the manager whose role is both broad and deep will normally welcome the opportunity to delegate, because it allows him to concentrate on the most important aspects of his job.

● does the culture allow people to extend their own jobs? Rigid lines of demarcation between departments and an atmosphere where becoming involved in another manager's area is regarded as unwarranted interference, are both likely to work against delegation, because they prevent managers from developing their jobs across functional lines.

Informal, often unplanned delegation frequently occurs when a manager, having gained control over his day-to-day responsibilities, seeks new challenges. The challenge may be a new product development, the creation of more efficient operating systems, the introduction of improved quality assurance procedures or indeed anything that builds upon his enthusiasm and his experience in the current job. If the manager is to devote the necessary time and mental energy to this new project, he *has* to delegate.

It can be valuable to find out how many managers have been able to follow this route. Analysis of the job function of a representative cross-section of managers may reveal, for example, that the role and job description of a high percentage has remained static for five years or more. If these managers have been unable to develop themselves over that period, it is unlikely that they will have been able to build up expertise in their subordinates by passing progressively more and more responsibility downwards.

Making delegation work can be a traumatic process, not least because in an organization with too many levels, it may leave some levels of management without a real function. Forcing them to delegate would mean expecting them to work themselves out of a job, which is unrealistic. Only if the rewards of doing this are greater than the risks will managers readily comply. It is essential to have a comprehensive plan of the new structure, and to make sure that everyone affected knows how that structure will work. While it may not be possible to provide details of the implications for individuals, it should normally be possible to spell out how many there will be at each level, the kind of person expected to fill each category and the overall process that will have to be gone through to create the new structure.

Effective delegation starts from the bottom up, not from the top down. Start from the lowest level and ask 'What are the maximum and minimum degrees of responsibility this level can take?' Don't rely solely on the opinions of superiors: the degree of responsibility the employee considers himself capable of assuming and is willing to assume will often surprise you. His peers may also have useful comments. This exercise provides reference points for the job (though not for the ability of its occupant). To put it another way, it defines the length of the rope by which the job is tethered, and how elastic the rope is. The same process should be repeated for each successive level in the hierarchy, from junior supervisor to board member.

In most companies this will automatically and swiftly lead to the conclusion that one or more layers of management are unnecessary. The resulting slimmer structure will not only save on salary bills, but also improve communications and enrich jobs to an extent normally beyond the capacity of the individual manager acting on his own.

The value of defining maximum and minimum levels of responsibility in each job is that it allows for varying ability and enthusiasm in successive job holders. The unit manager may allow a new recruit to operate at only the minimum level of responsibility at first, gradually delegating more and more to him. This progressive upgrading of delegation is much easier where both manager and subordinate understand the ground rules and the level of responsibility they are aiming at. It also provides a useful measure for positioning people in pay grades and for regular performance appraisal.

What the individual manager can do Delegation works in two ways. On the one hand, you want senior management to delegate more responsibility to you; on the other, you can delegate some of your job to your subordinates, as part of their personal development programme.

In seeking delegated responsibility from above you should:

● be honest with yourself about how ready you are for particular responsibilities. Don't try to run before you can walk; but don't be afraid to walk pretty fast.

● prepare a plan to take on specific new responsibilities, as suggested under 'General points' above

● when you have a performance appraisal, come prepared with suggestions of how additional responsibility would help you develop your management skills. Enlist the aid of the personnel department beforehand, to gain additional support for your proposals.

● if you are given new responsibility, make sure that you obtain the authority that goes with it. Responsibility without authority means that you get the blame when things go wrong, yet have little or no influence on the outcome. For this reason you must ensure that the limits of your new responsibility and authority are clearly set out and agreed between you and your superior.

● find a top management mentor, if you can, who will delegate tasks to you outside the normal activities of your functional area. Look for a senior manager who knows the company well, has an interest in developing keen younger managers and who might be able to use a 'runner' at your level. A mentoring relationship can be very intense, very demanding on both participants, but most people who have experienced it find it rewarding. Surveys in the United States suggest that, on average, people who have been mentored reach middle management two years ahead of people who have not. You can find a suitable mentor by first making yourself visible in your company. Take maximum advantage of meetings with senior management by volunteering to do presentations and reports. Make sure you are assigned to projects which have the support and involvement of top management. You can select the highly valued project from the inconsequential by identifying the one most relevant to the corporation's goals. If these are not clear, look carefully at the person leading the project; you usually know who is on the way up in the senior ranks. After you have built up a favourable reputation in your company, you can directly approach your potential mentor and persuade him that he will benefit as much as you from the relationship.

In delegating to your own subordinates:

● remember the difference between delegation and abdication. Abdication is passing responsibility to someone else and then forgetting about it; delegation is passing on immediate responsibility, yet retaining overall responsibility. Delegating something to someone else does not mean you should not remain closely involved in it.

● always be available to talk over the progress of delegated projects. Never let the employee feel he has been cast adrift. Although some people may rise to the challenge, others are likely to be disoriented by the experience.

● don't seize the reins back again too quickly. Let people learn from their own mistakes and help them pick up the pieces, if need be. Every time you take responsibility back it is your failure as much as that of the employee concerned.

A POSITIVE ATTITUDE TOWARDS RISK TAKING

What the chief executive can do To repeat from the previous chapter, the business schools can be blamed for producing generations of MBAs who are superb analysts but poor decision makers. These people have been taught that good management means analysing and planning to eliminate risk – a philosophy which has been warmly embraced in conservative companies where progress is a reward of avoiding failure rather than of creating success.

The problem with the analytical approach to management is that it is not the way that the best managers manage. One of the most perceptive analyses of top management decision making was conducted by Harvard assistant professor Daniel J. Isenberg, who debunks the assumption that successful senior managers are 'rational, purposeful and decisive'. Most successful senior managers, he asserts, do not closely follow the classical rational model of first clarifying goals, assessing the situation, formulating options, estimating likelihoods of success, making their decision, and only then taking action to implement the decision. Nor do top managers select one problem at a time to solve, as the rational model implies.

Instead of having precise goals and objectives, successful senior executives have general overriding concerns and think more often about how to do things than about what is being accomplished. They rely heavily on a mix of intuition and disciplined analysis in their decision making, and incorporate their action on a problem into their diagnosis of it.

In other words, successful management is more about doing than about thinking. By becoming actively involved in implementing the solutions to problems or opportunities, while the solution is still being worked out, the effective manager gains a much more realistic, hands-on understanding and is able to deal with the matter much more quickly. In the end, effective management involves a balance between analysis and action. It is, for example, a truism that a dynamic manager with a so-so product is more likely to succeed than a bureaucratic manager with a brilliant product..

The winning company needs to establish an environment where intelligent risk taking is both natural and expected. The first step here is to devise and publicize a policy for risk taking. The policy should establish:

- high rewards for high career risks.
- clear guidelines on the manner and degree of risk acceptable.

In the typical British company, the prospect of transfer to a loss-making subsidiary is enough to send managers into catalepsy. The move is unlikely to involve much in the way of increased salary – the ailing company cannot afford it – and the chances are high of ending up jobless if the enterprise folds. Promises of transfer elsewhere in such circumstances are not believed. Even if the promise is accepted at face value, the likelihood of the manager being able to assume a similar or equal job should the subsidiary fail is low; he is at best likely to be shunted aside where he cannot do any harm. In most British companies a manager would have to be foolhardy to take such a risk.

Changing this pattern, which may well have been ingrained into the culture by dint of practical experience, demands a change in the reward system. First, the degree of career risk needs to be reduced by a genuine acceptance by top management that one or two failures in high-risk projects should not be a black mark, and may actually equip a manager better for further ventures than colleagues who have not experienced such a baptism of fire. (It is noticeable that many of the most successful entrepreneurs are people whose first companies have failed, and who have learnt from their failures).

Second, it has to be recognized that it is harder to turn an ailing company or department into a winner than to keep a winner winning. The manager, or indeed the skilled non-management employee, in an ailing operation should be rewarded by an incentive scheme based on the impact he makes in improving results. In addition, the amount of the incentive should be commensurate with the degree of career risk he is taking. The assumption that the average level of bonus must be greater in successful units than in unsuccessful ones does not always hold water. The critical measurement is the degree of improvement made over the incentive period. In other words, the larger the carrot, the more readily will the best manager accept the challenge of the turnaround.

The same philosophy applies even more strongly to the new venture. To the managers selected to run the project, the game must be worth the candle. To most British companies the idea of providing managers with equity capital in such circumstances is still anathema, yet few incentives are so powerful. Profit-based incentives are a more common alternative, but less effective because they are short-term. The typical start-up is cash-hungry in its early years; profitability is held down in favour of growth. Focusing on profit too early is not in the long-term interests of the company, yet the incentive scheme (if any) will normally encourage the manager to follow that route. The rewards to both company and the new project managers are greatest when they are focused on the long term, i.e. through growth in equity value.

Third, it is essential to break the pattern of punishing failure where managers have done all (and more) that could be expected of them. The best way of doing this is by example – the very way in which the negative pattern was established. If top management recognizes that both a new venture and a chronically ill enterprise may well fail, it can make realistic contingency plans for redeploying the talent that may be released.

Unfortunately, what normally happens is that both top management and the manager appointed to the high-risk venture are trapped by their own machismo. Top management is afraid to talk about failure to the unit manager because it does not wish to suggest a lack of confidence in his ability to do the job. The unit manager himself dare not bring up the subject for fear of being regarded as lacking commitment or drive. As a result, the issue is avoided by both sides until it is too late. Each side then feels it has been let down by the other, making the task of rehabilitating the manager even more difficult. Discussing the issue of failure openly, at the start, clears the path for the creation of alternative paths into which these managers can be switched. It needs only a handful of examples of people who have been switched to real jobs with high visibility and high promotion potential for the message to get through.

Guidelines on the extent to which risks may be taken will vary according to circumstance, but there must be underlying principles on which the decisions to go ahead or step back will depend. Giving employees an insight into these principles will both encourage them to come forward with ideas and will head off unacceptable risk taking.

In effect, such a policy statement opens up top management's thinking and attitudes towards risk. This impression can be strengthened or weakened by the action that top management takes. There is little point in telling people lower down that they must be more adventurous, if top management itself is not prepared to make significant calculated risks itself. When it does so, it should ensure that it explains why it is doing so, the extentive groundwork, for example, that has gone into market research and planning, and what is at stake – the upside and downside risks involved. The more top management can put across such explanations in person, giving managers the opportunity to ask questions, the more likely it is to establish a viable model of risk taking for them to follow.

What the individual manager can do   It's surprising how few managers at junior and middle levels understand the nature of business risk. Typically they equate it with daring leaps into the blue, with staking fortunes on a gamble. While some companies do operate in that manner (usually not for very long), the normal business risk has as much of the risk taken out of it as top management can remove. Successful companies don't avoid risk, they control and limit it by painstaking preparation. You can adopt the same approach both to your department's operations and, by extension, to your career development.

First, however, let's look at your attitude towards risk. Answer the following three questions yourself, then ask your spouse or a close friend whether they agree with your perception of yourself.

● When you are offered a gift horse do you...?

   (a) *refuse it point blank*

(b) *look carefully at it before accepting*
(c) *grab it and look for the snags later*

● If you were given £10 to bet on a horse would you put it on...?

(a) *none: I'd just pocket it*
(b) *the six-to-one favourite*
(c) *the fifty-to-one outsider*

● Do you have...?

(a) *insurance policies for just about everything*
(b) *insurance for the disasters that would hurt most*
(c) *no insurance you don't legally have to*

If you chose (a) each time you are likely to be somewhat risk averse. If you chose (b) you are probably fairly well balanced in your attitude to risk. If you chose (c) you are probably prone to take excessive or wild risks.

Within the range of tasks and opportunities that present themselves in the large company, all three attitudes may be appropriate at one time or another. The flexible manager knows when to be cautious, when to take a considered gamble. Experience may teach you that skill in the long term, but you can also do a lot to teach yourself. You can, for example:

● train yourself or obtain training in risk analysis. A variety of techniques is now available to help managers work through the logic of complex problems until they can match risk against potential reward with reasonable confidence. Unfortunately, very few companies employ these techniques even at top management level.

● do your homework. Probably the biggest single reason for the failure of new products is inadequate market research. As a general rule, 'If something is critical to the success of a project, test it until you are sure your assumptions are right. Then go back and check them again.' You will never remove all the risk from a new venture, but you can greatly improve the odds.

● spread your risks. Never stake too much on high-risk ventures, but don't be afraid to throw in the occasional long shot if the downside risk is relatively small and the potential rewards very high. In reality, the risk here is high only if the project is measured on its own; set against a total programme it may be negligible.

- involve others in your risk taking, not to spread the blame if things go wrong, but to reduce the risk by getting their input and evaluation
- always go into a risk expecting to win, but don't be crushed by failure
- make sure more senior managers understand the risks you are taking – and what you are doing to try and negate the risks. They may not protect your back if things go wrong, but they are less likely to wield the knife themselves.
- always have a contingency plan, to limit the damage if things do go wrong – and to deal with the extra sales if they go much better than predicted.

You can encourage a positive attitude towards controlled risk taking among your subordinates by encouraging them to make adventurous suggestions. Then let them try some – even if you are sure they will fail. Choose ideas that cannot do much harm if they go wrong, but which are likely to provide them with a good learning experience. You may be pleasantly surprised when they make their suggestion work.

Explain to your subordinates how the company evaluates risk, how it reduces risk and what risk you consider acceptable. Involve them when you evaluate risk so that they can observe and learn from your way of thinking.

GENERALIST MANAGERS

What the chief executive can do In tomorrow's corporation, narrow functional specializations are dangerous for both employees and employers. For the employee there is the constant danger of skills becoming obsolete; of being directed down a narrow path that becomes narrower and narrower until it disappears altogether. For the employer, there is a loss of flexibility, an inability to rotate managers according to actual and predicted needs.

In *The Winning Streak* we found that the successful companies tended to provide employees with general management experience early in their careers. Less successful companies allowed people to rise through a functional hierarchy – sales, production, R&D, finance and so on – before giving them exposure to broader management problems. The drawback with the latter approach is that these managers suddenly have to unlearn twenty years' management experience, at a time when their ability to absorb change may be on the wane. Not surprisingly, the failure rate – measured in terms of both understanding and effective management action – is high.

General management expertise can be developed early on in a number of ways. One is to deliberately create learning experiences for young managers. Electronics giant Philips, for example, encourages young managers to collaborate in small teams to make recommendations on real problems facing the company.

The Brazilian subsidiary of US beverage company Heublein International Management Corporation has made such experiences permanent. It developed a form of organization where a very slim management structure obliged every functional manager to have responsibility for something outside his normal areas of expertise. The administration and information manager, for example, also takes the responsibility for organizing the priorities of distribution, as head of a committee set up for the purpose. Younger managers from other areas of the company participate in the decision making of a completely different area from their normal department.

The success of this approach led Heublein subsequently to appoint a small team as managing director of one of its main production units. When the previous managing director was promoted, none of the three functional heads below him had enough general management experience to step into his shoes without significant learning problems. Yet all had the potential to advance in the company. Heublein's innovative solution was to give the responsibility to them all. The final authority within the team rotated between its three members every six months, allowing the company to observe each of them at work in the hot seat. All three managers developed their general management abilities rapidly.

Another way of providing people with early exposure to general management issues is to encourage young managers to suggest projects they can pursue, which will oblige them to break out of the straitjacket of their own functional specialization and comprehend the broader corporate perspective.

A third approach is to encourage mentoring of young managers by 'elder statesmen' in middle and senior management. Formalize what is now an *ad hoc* series of relationships into broader opportunities for all high flyers. The time spent on mentoring by the elder manager provides an invaluable insight for the young manager into how and why key decisions are made, into how to handle corporate politics and how to gain and use authority and power. The combination of mentoring and a practical project is a very powerful method of management development, which should, in the long term, create a cadre of junior and middle managers whose understanding of the company spreads well beyond the confines of their own job.

What the individual manager can do   One of the worst career mistakes you can make today if you have ambitions to reach top management is to become trapped in a single specialist function. On average, the career progress of a person who passes the age of forty with experience of only one functional area is likely to come to a halt several years before that of the person who has acquired broad experience of several functions.

If your company does not automatically provide you with broader experience, you will have to make the opportunity yourself. If you are in, say, production or R&D, ask for a temporary transfer to sales. Your background knowledge is likely to be welcomed – they don't get many volunteers with your experience.

Do read about other functions. You can, for example, take distance learning courses in accounting for non-financial managers or in personnel management, even if those are not your functional area. Most companies will pay part or all of the cost of such courses, if they do not take you away from your job.

Get involved in multi-disciplinary projects, where you can rub shoulders with managers who have other specializations. At the very least, you will learn to understand their jargon.

As we suggested in the chapter on leadership, do take advantage of the opportunities for developing broader management expertise that are offered by professional bodies and voluntary organizations. The broader perspective you develop may help you identify niches in the company that will give you the opportunity to gain general management experience. For example, could you make use of advances in information technology to take your company into some new form of on-line customer service?

If, in the end, there is no prospect of gaining generalist management experience in your formative years as a manager – move on. Most people learn all they are going to and make their most significant contributions to a job within the first four years. Thereafter, you need to move up, move out or expand the job to take in major new elements.

3 Winning through control

Few businesses die because they have no controls. They die either because they have the wrong controls or because they have too many. The small business (and sometimes the big one) that pays so much attention to customer service that cashflow is neglected is a common enough phenomenon. So too is the bureaucratic company that pulls the reins so tight that it throttles the horse. The more effective your controls are, the greater the autonomy you can afford.

What these companies have forgotten is that controls are only of value if they assist them in their primary purpose of serving their markets profitably. The problem is compounded by the fact that the company and the environment in which it operates both change. But few companies systematically evaluate their control systems to ensure they still fit top management's objectives. As Tom Peters, co-author of *In Search of Excellence*, writes in the introduction to the US edition of *The Winning Streak*, 'A few [controls] that are believed are much more effective than numerous controls that are honored principally in the breach.'

Worse still, the systems themselves can change in unplanned, often unexpected ways as people divert them to their own objectives. And the more complex they become, the greater the likelihood of failure – or to put it another way, the larger the system, the closer to infinity is the number of things that can conceivably go wrong.

Before you can start to control your controls, you have to know where you are now – whether the controls you have are working for or against maximum efficiency, and whether you have all the controls you need. In particular, you must decide what is the key information you need to monitor the business. The following questions will form a starting point for evaluating the broad status of your control systems.

GENERAL QUESTIONS

1   How often does top management change the control system?

> *frequently*
> *occasionally*

2   List the formal controls that your company applies to you. What proportion of them is designed to help *you* do your job rather than tell someone else what you are doing?

> *all or most*
> *about half*
> *very few*
> *none*

3   Are the same basic controls applied across the company?

4   Do you fully understand the reasoning behind and need for ...?

> *all the controls*
> *most of the controls*
> *some of the controls*
> *none of the controls*

5   Are the control systems generally ...?

> *simple to operate*
> *fairly simple*
> *difficult*
> *in need of an expert to interpret them*

6   If you had the opportunity, what proportion of the control systems would you jettison tomorrow?

> *more than half*
> *a quarter to a half*
> *less than a quarter*
> *none*

7   Has anyone in the company ever tried to put the control systems into context for you as part of the overall corporate objectives?

8   Does top management have as its key controls...?

> *fewer than five critical measurements*
> *six to ten critical measurements*
> *more than ten critical measurements*

TIGHT CONTROLS ON FINANCE

9   Are tight financial controls the result of poor profit and cashflow generally in the company, or of a planned diversion of resources where they will do most good?

10   Which of the following statements is most accurate?

> *my company approves capital expenditure readily if there is a sufficiently large demonstrable saving to be made*
> *my company only ever approves capital expenditure reluctantly*
> *my company approves of capital expenditure – if the money's there*
> *my company hardly ever queries capital expenditure*

11   What, in your view is the primary purpose of financial controls in your company?

> *to hold expenditure down at any cost*
> *to act as an early warning system of financial problems*
> *to give top management the flexibility it needs to plan market responses*
> *to keep everyone down the line in line*

12   How much of the financial information you provide on a regular basis do you use in your job?

> *all*
> *most*
> *some*
> *none*

13   How much of the financial information you provide on a regular basis are you aware of more senior management using?

> *all*
> *most*

some
none

14   How closely are cash controls tied to personal reward?

very closely
loosely
very loosely
not at all

CONSTANT FEEDBACK OF RESULTS

15   How quickly are last month's figures consolidated and presented to top management?

within thirty-six hours
within seventy-two hours
within a week
a month or more

16   How far down the chain are those results communicated?

to all employees
down to supervisor level
to middle management
to senior management only

17   What proportion of junior managers know the profit and loss status of their department from week to week?

most
a few
none

18   Is management appraisal on other key criteria carried out...?

on a daily basis
six-monthly
annually
rarely, if ever

19   Do you always know how well you are performing in the areas that matter to your company?

20 Do you know what the controls that really matter to top management are?

CLOSE ATTENTION TO BUSINESS PLANNING

21 Is business planning in your company ...?

> *an ongoing affair, part of daily routine*
> *an annual event*
> *less frequent than annual*

22 Who gets involved in the financial side of business planning?

> *everyone*
> *all management and supervisory levels*
> *senior management/board members only*

23 How much personal ownership do you feel toward your portion of the business plan?

> *a good deal*
> *some*
> *none*

24 In a typical year does your company/department ...?

> *come out pretty close to plan*
> *miss plan by miles every time*

25 When actual sales fall below those predicted in the business plan, does your company typically ...?

> *keep changing the plan to fit the real world*
> *change the real world to fit the plan, by throwing in additional effort*
> *bury its head and hope for the best*

26 At the end of the financial year does your department typically ...?

> *push all possible expenses into the closing year on the basis that it was so bad a bit more won't matter*

push all possible expenses into the coming year on the basis that you have to do something to make the figures look better
present an accurate financial picture of events

HIGH STANDARDS

27   Does your company clearly state, for all employees, the general standards of performance it requires from them?

28   Are you personally clear about the *standards* of performance expected of you?

29   Does top management provide an example of high standards for others to follow?

30   Is there a company folklore – a set of anecdotes – that reinforces the standards expected of employees?

31   Do managers in your company react to sub-standard behaviour or performance by...?

jumping on the employee concerned then and there, whenever they see something wrong
storing up a catalogue of complaints until they have enough to confront the employee in a rap session
tolerating mal-performance until it either corrects itself or becomes sufficiently serious that action has to be taken

---

POINTS TO WATCH

Question 1: while it is true that constant change in the market requires corresponding change in the company and its organization, most useful controls will be fundamental to the business. If you answered that your company changes its controls frequently, it is an indication that the control systems are too complex. Simple controls rarely need much change, whatever happens outside the company.

Question 25: it's surprising how many managers instinctively choose the first alternative which is, in effect, equivalent to no planning.

Ideally the financial objectives of the plan should remain; only the means of achieving them should change, i.e. the second alternative is the only one that makes sense in term of winning.

Question31: you might think that managers should hold their peace on little things. After all, surely people become very irritated and resentful at constant nitpicking? The answer, as we shall see late in the chapter, is that, properly handled, constant vigilance by the manager is actually appreciated far more by his subordinates.

GENERAL POINTS

What the chief executive can do   Your answers to the questions above should have thrown some light on the overall status of your company's control systems and in particular whether they are helping or hindering the achievement of the company's objectives.

Before you can turn this information to practical use, however, it is necessary to dig several layers of detail deeper, by identifying the controls you have. That is, what do you control, how and why? Many controls will be written up in procedural manuals – these formal ones are the easy ones to list. Others, although informal, may be equally important, and usually fall into one of two categories. The first is the officially condoned control, an enforced norm that fits top management's view of how the world should be: for example, standards of dress or the layout of memos and letters, neither of which may be important enough to warrant a procedural memo, but which attract automatic comment if they are transgressed. The second is the unofficial controls that top management would not approve of, but which still flourish from convenience or habit. A typical example here might be the detailed personnel records many US managers maintain in their desk drawers. Because the formal record system purges most subjective data on data privacy grounds, foremen and supervisors tend to keep unofficial records to which they can refer. Attempts to stamp out these records almost invariably fail.

The length of your list may well surprise you. So, too, may the number of controls which are no longer relevant, or which have been completely diverted from their original and still valid purpose. One suggestion that surfaces from time to time but rarely, if ever, seems to be implemented, is that all formal controls should have a shelf life, a specific date beyond which they are automatically discarded unless specifically renewed. This is perhaps as good a test as any of their real need.

The list of controls can be analysed in a variety of other ways, to answer the following questions:

● whom are they intended to help, and do they achieve that objective?
● how frequently is this information gathered?
● do they work with or against the company culture?

It is surprising how many control systems do not actually control anything. They provide information, but the information is never used as the basis for action. Without a regular form of monitoring, action and feedback, such activities are counterproductive in that they waste effort that could be profitably employed elsewhere.

Effective control systems start at the lowest level of supervision. They provide the supervisor with the information he needs to establish what is going right and wrong in his department, where action needs to be taken, and where everything is running smoothly and intervention is not needed. It is essential that the supervisor accepts these systems as *his* systems, even if they have been designed as a factory or company standard. Whenever possible, he should also be responsible for gathering the data, too. An impersonal printout, delivered a week or more after the event, is of minimal value to him in maintaining or raising efficiency. He needs 'real-time' information under his own control.

Virtually all the information required by more senior levels of management should be extrapolated from that contained in the supervisor's system. Anything else should be closely examined to ensure that it really is essential. In general, the only useful information that does not emerge naturally from the effective control systems of lower layers in the organization is information required to comply with government regulations. Anything else is likely to be make-work. Certainly any information that has to be specially gathered for middle or senior management should be immediately suspect. There should indeed be a pyramid of management information, with the smallest quantity of information needed at the top and the most needed at the bottom.

Those controls that *are* clearly necessary may be exercised at the wrong frequency. Too frequent monitoring of what is going on can be as harmful as not checking enough. It ties management and supervisory time up in unproductive work, and can colour people's perception of all the controls they work with. The frequency, like the content, of controls has to be relevant to the person who operates it at the lowest as well as at the highest level.

In the few cases – and they will be few – where an employee has to operate controls or gather information not relevant to or useful in his immediate job, it is essential to explain to him why the information is needed and the problems that will be created if he gets it wrong or ignores it.

The issue of whether controls work with or against the company culture is important at a time of stability because controls that run against the grain will frequently give rise to unofficial systems. At a time of major change it is even more important, because managers can use control systems to change the culture. The design of financial controls, for example, can have a significant effect on a manager's behaviour. As long as they are accepted and endorsed by the people who have to operate them, new systems can create new behaviour and attitudes.

The problem lies in gaining this acceptance. For a start, this may be done by involving people in the development and maintenance of the systems that affect them. Ask them: What information do they need to do their job most effectively? What goes wrong most often? What aspects of the control systems appear pointless or excessive to them? In most cases they will have a much better idea than more senior managers of what controls are needed; in the rest of cases, it is incumbent upon the company to explain why the employees' perception is wrong.

Managers can reinforce the importance and hence the acceptance of control information by making a point of discussing it with the people who produce it, either to congratulate them for the smooth running of their departments or to question why something has gone wrong. In each case, it shows the employees that their efforts really are useful to more senior levels of management.

It also makes a great deal of sense to tie the control systems to the company's reward systems, i.e. to make sure that people are rewarded for following the rules rather than for ignoring them. Management by objectives has lost much of the popularity it had in the 1960s and early 1970s, as many companies found the results disappointing. However, the basic principles behind the concept of setting goals and evaluating how well people achieve them are still sound. What has been lacking in most cases of failure is realistic goals and efficient means of measurement. Good controls, which monitor critical aspects of corporate health, form the basis upon which objectives and measurements can be based. It is important, however, to ensure that the rewards relate to appropriate periods of time. For a manual worker, incentives may best be tied to a monthly cycle; for a manager, perhaps a year. For top management, a major element of the incentive package should be related to long-term performance.

Among other questions you can ask to measure the effectiveness of your control systems are:

● are the appropriate controls at the appropriate level? All too often it turns out that the control is exercised too high or too low in the organization. Too low, and the objectives may be lost entirely; too high, and implementation is patchy at best. Controls have to be 'hands on' to be truly effective.

● how frequent are nasty surprises? Good controls should avoid unexpected calamities. But preventing surprises is no excuse for overloading departments with controls they do not need. Part of the solution to the dilemma is to create an atmosphere where people who reveal errors they have made will not be punished if they also come up with the remedy. People in such organizations are less likely to be haunted by their mistakes. This kind of disclosure can release a great many of the pressures within an organization, allowing people to concentrate on constructive problem solving. A good test of how close your organization comes to this ideal is to tot up how often you have to say 'Why didn't you tell me?' – even once may be too often.

● what possible events would be disastrous for your company? These are the events – the nasty surprises – which the control systems should seek to prevent. You need to monitor what is happening sufficiently closely to take corrective action in good time, yet not so closely that the detail obscures the significant trends.

● is the information needed for each major control presented on a single sheet? To lead to immediate action, control information has to be simple and obvious, whether on the shopfloor or in the boardroom. Top management does not normally have the time to analyse pages of figures. It needs to see a brief summary from which it can extract at a glance what is going right or wrong,

what the significant trends are, and what corrective action is
already being taken.
● do you have a clear idea of what is happening in the divisions at
any moment? If not, then the information you are getting is
probably not the right information.

It takes a lot of hard work to ensure that controls are exercised in
a manner that allows the greatest useful autonomy but avoids lapsing
into anarchy. Regular examination of the control systems, both as a
whole and in their individual parts, will help prevent them becoming
malignant.

What the individual manager can do While you are inevitably
bound by company-wide control systems, you will almost certainly
operate a number of controls that relate solely to your department.
You can undertake a regular review of these controls, to ensure they
are still relevant and useful and that they mesh with the standard
company reporting systems. What documents do you send to other
departments? What do they need them for? Would it be more helpful
to them if the documents were designed in a different way, or had
more or less information? Ask your subordinates to list the information they gather for their own and other people's use. How much of
it *is* used?

If you cannot see the value of some of the information you have
to pass upwards, query it. Ask a senior manager to explain the uses
of the various controls and what could happen if they were not in
place. Share that knowledge with your subordinates or, better still,
get the senior manager to explain it to you all together. Like you, he
has a vested interest in ensuring that people in your department
accept and understand the controls they administer.

When you review the controls you operate, ask also for suggestions
on how they could be made simpler. Complexity in control systems
frequently implies woolly thinking rather than sophistication. If a
system isn't yet computerized, analysing it prior to programming is
an ideal time to ask fundamental questions about its purpose and
how that might be achieved more simply.

TIGHT CONTROLS ON FINANCE

What the chief executive can do   In the modern decentralized company, group headquarters is becoming more and more like a bank, taking profits as deposits and making loans in the form of capital investment and working capital. More and more your role is that of merchant banker, making sure the cash is loaned out to good credit risks, and hedging by balancing high-risk ventures with sure returns.

The merchant banking viewpoint allows you to create rules and policies regarding capital expenditure, investment and cashflow that are transparent to everyone who has to operate them. If all decisions are based on a projected return, it concentrates managers' minds wonderfully on the economic realities of their part of the business. It becomes very hard for them to justify any expenditure if they haven't a clear idea of where the costs and profits of their operations lie.

What the individual manager can do   Whatever the degree of financial autonomy you have within your company, you can still behave like an entrepreneur. Consider the cash invested in your department (whether in people or in plant) as a loan on an asset that has to be managed. How can you maximize the return on that asset?

The point is that controlling expenditure is not the same thing as cutting costs. Indeed, there are many situations where entrepreneurial asset management will require an increase in costs to create a greater return on investment. Just as an entrepreneur has to justify his idea and sell it to the merchant bank, so the unit manager must sell his investment to senior management. The value of this discipline is that it requires you to think consistently in profit terms. And that is a skill you will need increasingly as you climb the corporate hierarchy.

CONSTANT FEEDBACK OF RESULTS

What the chief executive can do   The three key characteristics of a good feedback system are speed, accuracy and relevance. A good starting point to check on the efficiency of the feedback system is the information coming to you. Even in a highly complex and diversified group the finance department should be able to deliver the key data from the previous week to you on Monday morning. If it can't, you need either better computers or a new finance director.

If you can have that data within thirty-six or forty-eight hours, there is no practical reason why staff at lower levels should not all have their requirements for feedback satisfied within three or four days. As for accuracy and relevance, the simplest and most practical test is probably whether the feedback is used. An investigation into what people actually use may well enable you to cut out a lot of irrelevant reports, and condense others to a few sheets.

An interesting description of the importance of fast, accurate and relevant feedback in your own day-to-day decision making comes from Dr Peter Keen, a management consultant and former visiting professor at London Business School. He explains:

> Information float is the gap between something happening and the manager finding out about it. Money float – uncollected funds, uncashed cheques and so on – has an obvious cost. The cost of information float is less visible, but can be very expensive. For example, a pricing problem may show up as an increase in inventory levels six months later, on the quarterly financial reports, because the reporting cycle is organized around *post hoc* financials instead of providing early warning signals.... Reports based on the financials rarely provide timely operating indicators that can alert the manager to potential problems early enough to react to them.

What the individual manager can do In principle, everyone who does a task that influences a key area of the company's performance needs regular feedback on how he is doing. Even the cleaning staff need to know whether they are doing a good or poor job of emptying the waste-paper baskets or polishing the floor.

However, relatively few companies go so far as to provide financial feedback all down the line. Most of those that do confine it to annual or bi-annual briefings. Yet the potential benefits of involving all employees in the financial fortunes of their operating unit on a monthly or fortnightly basis are enormous. For one thing, this level of frequency allows them to relate their own efforts directly to the unit's financial performance. They can see where the breakdown of a poorly maintained machine, or the need to retype a major report, caused a loss in productivity and profitability. They can see how absenteeism holds up production and delays the sending out of invoices needed to maintain cashflow. All of this obliges them to take more responsibility for their own jobs.

Conducting these briefings is your responsibility and it requires you to ensure that you have the information to pass on. If the company's normal reporting systems do not feed it back to you, ask the finance department to generate a regular special report. You need that information anyway, if you are to take proper control of what is happening in your department. Without it, you are a not a manager, but a minder.

CLOSE ATTENTION TO BUSINESS PLANNING

What the chief executive can do   Being the strategist-in-chief of your company is your most important role. You have not only to oversee the development of viable strategic plans that meet the demands both of the marketplace and of the corporate mission, but to make sure that the strategies so painstakingly worked out are put into practice. That is probably the hardest part of all.

You can improve or maintain the effectiveness of your company's planning by ensuring that it is:

- both top down and bottom up. It should involve all levels of the organization in successive waves of discussion and rethinking until everyone understands and is committed to their part of the common goal. Bitter experience has taught many companies that top down decision making in strategy does not work on its own.
- carried out by line managers, *not by corporate planning staff*. In a long and detailed article entitled 'The new breed of strategic planner', *Business Week* (17 September 1984) reported 'a fundamental shift of corporate power [where] line managers in one company after another are successfully challenging the hordes of professional planners and are forcing them from positions of influence'. Companies that had previously constructed plans for each subsidiary at headquarters have slashed their central planning staff and moved them out to the operating units, where they now report to line management. The planner, says *Business Week*, is now being used as 'a 'catalyst for change – not to do the planning for each business unit'. The reason for this change is that centralized planning just didn't work. Explains *Business*

Week: 'Few of the supposedly brilliant strategies concocted by planners were successfully implemented.' Analytical, formula-bound planning turned out to be unexpectedly transparent to competitors – they could do the same calculations – while the welter of detail churned out by corporate planning departments often became more of a hindrance than a help to line managers responsible for making the business work. 'The end result', says *Business Week*, 'is that planners disrupt a company's ability to assess the outside world and to create strategies for a sustainable competitive advantage.... As strategic planning became less of a creative thinking exercise and more of a bureaucratic process, its original purpose was lost....' The higher up the corporate hierarchy, the greater the proportion of a manager's time should be spent thinking about the business. To let someone else do the number crunching and the routine data gathering is delegation; to let someone else do the thinking is abdication.

● able to combine detail with flexibility. What are we going to do? Why? and What will we do if it goes wrong? are the three essential questions the planning process has to answer. The aim of planning detail is not to lay down rigid rules, but to permit the manager to measure whether he is on target, to assess when and where things are going wrong and to take corrective action before a potential problem becomes a real one. All too often, however, the objectives of the plan become subordinated at operational level to achieving detailed targets which are already obsolete. Hence effective planning also is:

● a continuous process, rather than a once-a-year event. The planning cycle is in reality a number of interlinked cycles rotating at different speeds. Think of them if you will as a series of cogs or gears. The largest cycle – the five- or ten-year plan – turns slowly, but its slightest movement causes the smallest cog to rotate rapidly. Conversely, it takes a lot of activity for the smallest cog to move the largest.

The art is to link all these cycles together so that they all keep moving in co-ordination. If one stops they all stop – or else the cogs become completely disconnected, with each planning cycle spinning on its own unco-ordinated way. The only way to keep all the cogs working together is to engage all managers in planning, all the time. To monitor, to evaluate and to review are essential parts of every manager's job. What has to be added is the ability to think beyond the routine cycle of information (which should be provided by the control systems) to the implications of external events and to the generation of alternative ways of doing things. Stopping routine work once a year or even once a month to take time out to consider such issues means, in effect, that managers are abdicating this responsibility for the rest of the time. What they should be doing is conducting the process as a constant part of their routine work. Only then can the planning process become dynamic.

A specious but common argument against continuous planning is that it occupies too much managerial time. In reality, it is almost impossible for top management to spend too much time planning, while at lower levels the regular discipline of strategic thinking and the preparatory work done as part of routine daily operations mean that the consolidation of a forward annual plan is a rapid affair achieving a high degree of consensus and commitment. In many cases the action needed to put the next cycle of the plan into effect will have been started long before the plan itself is formally agreed, because the pattern or shape of the plan is already visible to all concerned. The resulting speed of implementation contrasts starkly with the situation in so many companies, where all significant action comes to a halt while the 'great debate' drags on over which numbers senior management will place its chips on this time around.

Effective planning depends in the end upon educating and motivating the whole management team to take an active part in the process and upon giving them the freedom to do so. It also depends upon embracing change as an inevitable and largely beneficial part of the planning process. In particular, it recognizes that plans can and should be changed to take advantage of opportunity rather than just to deal with adversity. That requires open discussion, an acceptance not only that the plan, once made, *can* be criticized, but that it *should* be criticized, tested, refined and remade in a never-ending cycle. Allowing inadequate or obsolete plans to lumber on, simply because a manager has a lot of notional capital or prestige tied up in them, is a recipe for disaster. Managers must be encouraged to criticize their own plans and projects, to seek out the flaws before others do that for them.

It can be a painful process. But once used to the intellectual stimulation and challenge involved in the iconoclastic approach to planning, few managers will willingly work in any other way.

What the individual manager can do   If you have been invited to play in the concert, bring your own instrument. Or, to put it another way, if planning is to be a participative exercise, participate. You can do so by:

- preparing well-argued, fully-costed proposals for inclusion or discussion at planning meetings
- evaluating your department against top management's short- and long-term objectives. How could it fit in more closely with the overall direction in which top management is pushing the organization? Come prepared with positive ideas on changes that can be made.
- learning from past mistakes. It is rare for any business plan to work out exactly as expected. By the time it comes to conduct the post-mortem, however, everyone's attention is focused on the next planning cycle and the opportunity to dissect what happened in detail is lost. You can overcome this problem by maintaining a diary of deviations from plan and what caused them. Look for patterns and trends, for silly mistakes that could have been avoided, for excessive optimism and pessimism, and apply what you find to your input to next year's plan.

HIGH STANDARDS

What the chief executive can do   It's amazing what ordinary people can do, if only they are convinced that someone they respect believes them capable of it. Simply raising the standards you expect of people can produce remarkable results. This is partly because they want to prove to you that you are not underestimating their capabilities. It is also because high standards go hand in hand with high status. Put another way, people feel better working for a company with a high-quality image.

On the other hand, another reason why management by objectives so often fails is that it is not in any line manager's interest to set truly ambitious goals. If he does and fails to achieve them, he does not normally receive a pat on the back for what he did achieve. On the contrary, he is almost certain to receive a lower rating in his subsequent performance appraisal than would have been the case had he set himself merely adequate goals. This conspiracy of mediocrity inevitably includes his boss, who has no wish to be identified as the person whose subordinates missed their targets.

For this reason, it is important that the demand for high standards is all-pervasive. It is no good insisting on high standards of customer service if the product quality is dreadful. That's a little like expecting someone to buy a gold watch with a cheap mechanism, or a quality car with plastic upholstery.

Look at the activities that matter in your company. Ask yourself: Do we have clear standards for each of these? If you do, how demanding are those standards? One very good indicator of the standard of your company's standards is its attitude towards quality control. In manufacturing, for example, by far the majority of companies expect a percentage of their production to be less than perfect. They take the view that beyond a certain point, the returns from investment in preventing faults diminish rapidly until they cost more than the product is worth. It took the Japanese to demonstrate conclusively that wiping out those last percentage points actually reduces costs by raising overall productivity. The number of companies applying total quality control in the UK is still lamentably small, however. Total quality control is equally applicable to service functions.

Near perfection is regularly achievable and the benefits that flow from it are enormous: in marketplace reputation, in employee motivation, in the value that the customer places upon it and how much he will be prepared to pay. Companies which have invested heavily in total quality control find that even the relationship with their suppliers, who may until then have had to put up with extensive rejects, may eventually show radical improvement. Not only does a conscientious supplier appreciate working for a customer with consistent standards, but the investment he has to make in raising standards for this customer has knock-on benefits in his relationship with other customers.

As a general rule, the standards required of all employees of excellent companies take very good as a starting point, and then expect a bit more. This is a simple but effective means of extracting extraordinary performance from ordinary people. It seems to work particularly well when it is reinforced by example, in the company newspaper, in discussions with executives and of course, in the behaviour of top management itself. Start by giving people small fences to jump and keep raising the height.

What the individual manager can do   One measurement of your ability as a leader is the level of consistent performance you obtain from your subordinates. To achieve a consistently high level of performance you have to establish, both to yourself and to them, what standards you expect of them. The wise manager neither assumes that most people will automatically set themselves high targets, nor that they will automatically settle for the lowest they can get away with, but that they will settle for a comfortable personal equilibrium. Your task is to raise the threshold of that equilibrium, by showing them not only that they can perform at a higher level, but that it is more satisfying to do so.

The place to start is with yourself. Are the standards you set for yourself merely comfortable, or do they force you to additional effort well beyond your job description? When asked to do a one-off task by more senior management, do you aim to get it out of the way as quickly as possible or do you see it as an opportunity to show how good a job you can do? Before you can expect others to heed your exhortations to higher standards of performance, you have to be seen to be equally tough on yourself. As every good general knows, there are far fewer complaints about the food if the officers eat the same as the troops.

The standards you establish within your department should be twofold. First, there should be general standards of work that everyone is expected to adhere to. Second, there must be individual standards, which use the general standards as a starting point for even higher levels of expected performance to fit the individual and his job. Talk over these standards with the people concerned. Get them to write them down; find ways to stretch them.

While not all standards are quantifiable (how do you measure a receptionist's helpfulness, for example?) they do provide you with a yardstick against which to measure everything that goes on in your department – from how quickly enquiries are dealt with to the quality of production. You can reinforce those standards by your presence, by constantly checking and monitoring and, most importantly, by reacting whenever the standards are missed or exceeded. Prompt praise when people do even better than the best you had expected makes them feel that their efforts have been worthwhile. Gradually you may be able to raise the standards farther as people become used to performing at this higher level. By the same token, prompt reaction, pointing out when and where people's performance has failed to reach the high standard required, leaves them in no doubt about how serious you are. Don't be tempted to ignore the minor faults and failures because it would be too much trouble to deal with them; that is exactly the attitude you are trying to dispel among your subordinates. No error is so insignificant that it does not deserve comment.

Finally, you can ensure that everyone has the support they need to attain the high standards you require of them. Involve the employees themselves in identifying what they need to do their job better. Then do everything you can to take care of those needs. Once a secretary has the word processor she says she needs to increase the quantity and quality of her output, for example, she will be under moral obligation to prove that she was right. By gradually removing all the excuses, and by providing an example yourself, you leave your subordinates with little choice but to raise their sights in their own job – their own self-respect will demand it.

4 Winning through involvement

In *The Winning Streak* we found that the successful companies extracted a remarkable degree of commitment and loyalty from employees at all levels. The reason seems to be that these companies manage to involve their employees closely with the organization and its aims. Try the following questions to test how well your company does in terms of involvement.

GENERAL QUESTIONS

1a How many of the staff in your department would turn up voluntarily to help with a crisis elsewhere in the company, for no extra pay?

> *all*
> *most*
> *a few*
> *none*

b Would you?

2 Are tales of high devotion to duty in your firm ...?

> *so common as to be unremarkable*
> *fairly frequent*
> *rare*
> *unheard of*

3 How would you describe the degree of commitment among top management?

high
modest
low
nil

4   How would you describe the degree of commitment among middle and junior management?

high
modest
low
nil

5   How would you describe the degree of commitment among ordinary employees?

high
modest
low
nil

6   How hard does the company try to involve employees in improving productivity?

very hard
moderately
not at all

7   How hard does the company try to involve employees in improving profitability?

very hard
moderately
not at all

PRIDE IN OWNERSHIP

8   Do most employees feel there is some status in working for your company?

9   Are 'quality', 'skill' or "craftmanship' frequently used words in the company vocabulary?

10a If all or most employees can buy shares preferentially, how many of those eligible actually do so?

> *more than two-thirds*
> *more than one-third*
> *less than one-third*

b How many of those employees sell their shares as soon as possible?

> *more than two-thirds*
> *more than one-third*
> *less than one-third*

11 How much information about share value and performance is communicated to lower-level employees?

> *a lot*
> *some*
> *very little*
> *none*

12 How much effort does management put into reinforcing and developing people's pride in the firm?

> *a lot*
> *some*
> *very little*
> *none*

13 How much effort does top management put into genuine employee participation?

> *a lot*
> *some*
> *very little*
> *none*

14a Do the employees feel they are consulted on all the issues that concern them?

b Has your company asked employees how much and in what areas they *want* to be involved?

15   How do the trade union officials regard your company's chief executive?

> *as an honest man who genuinely wants their involvement*
> *as an honest man who doesn't want their involvement*
> *as a dishonest schemer*

HIGH DEGREE OF COMMUNICATIONS

16   Many companies say they have an open-door policy. Is your company's ...?

> *totally open: anyone can see top management if they feel they have a reason*
> *fairly open: anyone can see top management if the executive secretaries feel they have a reason*
> *fairly closed: it's difficult to see top management without going through formalities*
> *very closed: getting into Fort Knox would be easier*

17   When does your company break bad news?

> *as soon as top management suspects there may be a problem*
> *as soon as top management knows there is a problem*
> *when the decision on what to do is being taken*
> *when the decision on what to do has been taken*
> *at the last possible moment*

18   A new chief executive asks a meeting of middle managers for their honest criticisms of the company. Three managers stand up and deliver withering blasts. Would those managers ...?

> *be invited to prepare more detailed reports supporting what they have to say, or invited on to an action committee*
> *be given a polite hearing, but not invited to take their comments further*
> *be quietly transferred to Bangui or Ulan Bator*
> *be publicly fired*

19 Does your company believe that...?

employees can be trusted with very delicate trade secrets, if they
understand the importance of living up to that trust
employees can be trusted with a lot of information, but nothing
commercially sensitive
employees should never be trusted with anything you wouldn't
want the competition to know

20 Is your company's employee newspaper regarded as...?

an open forum for debate, with constructive criticism welcomed
a useful method for top management to explain its thinking to
people lower in the hierarchy
just a social diary, with minimal business information
just a management mouthpiece

21 When did your company last carry out a communications audit?

within the past two years
within the past five years
what's a communications audit?

HIGH PAY AND/OR INCENTIVES

22 In general does your company pay ...?

higher salaries than the competition
about the same salaries as the competition
lower salaries than the competition

23a Do incentive payments make up...?

30 per cent or more of senior managers' income
15 to 30 per cent of senior managers' income
less than 15 per cent of senior managers' income
we don't have any incentive payments at management levels

b Are they linked to...?

total company performance
performance of the unit

performance of the individual
a mixture of the above

c   Are the incentive targets realistically achievable?

PROMOTION FROM WITHIN

24   What percentage of appointments to middle and senior management positions in your company come from within?

almost all
more than two-thirds
less than two-thirds

TRAINING

25   In your company where does responsibility for training rest?

with the line managers
jointly between line managers and the training department
with the training department
it's the employee's own problem

26   Does your company train managers mainly by ...?

deliberately putting them in situations where they will learn by doing
sending them on courses
it doesn't train its managers

THE SOCIAL SIDE OF WORK

27   At management levels in your company's culture, is work regarded ...?

as fun – as a source of personal fulfilment
as an unpleasant necessity
as something to be avoided wherever possible

GENUINE RESPECT FOR THE INDIVIDUAL

28 Does your company have a clear policy regarding the welfare of employees?

29 An employee in your unit suddenly suffers a substantial drop in his performance. Although warned about it, he seems unable to improve. Does your company...?

> *automatically assume that the problem may be domestic or health-related and attempt to provide help*
> *keep on giving warnings in the hope he will sort himself out*
> *go through the dismissal procedure as quickly as possible*

30 If faced with a serious problem, where cutbacks are necessary, does your company...?

> *make every attempt to redeploy staff and pay for professional assistance in outplacement of those for whom it cannot find alternative work*
> *make some attempts to find alternative work*
> *chop and be damned*

POINTS TO WATCH:

Question 17: if you chose the first answer, you are likely to be creating unnecessary anxiety among the employees. You can actually create problems by making people worry about things that are unlikely to happen.

Question 24: promotion from within is generally good news, but you can have too much of a good thing. Winning streak companies ensure that there is always some new blood, even if there is no more than 10 or 15 per cent.

GENERAL POINTS

Good working relationships depend on four key qualities: trust, respect, understanding and competence. Each of the issues we shall deal with later in this chapter relates to one or more of these qualities. If any of these is missing, the relationship is likely to be flawed.

What the chief executive can do If serious deficiencies are revealed by the questions above, you should ask yourself the following further questions:

● does the company's behaviour truly merit the trust and respect of employees?
● does the company make genuine and adequate efforts to promote understanding?
● does the company demonstrate the competence that allows people to feel that top management knows what it is doing?

If you can be honest with yourself in answering these questions, you are probably already a good way towards increasing the level of involvement of your employees.

It is, however, relatively easy to be fooled into thinking that employees are more committed to the organization than is actually the case. Indeed, the higher up the company hierarchy you go, the less likely you are to gain an accurate picture. In most companies nobody in his right mind would tell a senior manager bluntly that this or that aspect of the company's policy or practice stinks – unless he is a trade union representative, in which case his opinion will immediately be discounted as 'lacking in objectivity'. Even if people do feel encouraged to speak up, the greater the number of hierarchical levels they have to span to do so, the more what they say is likely to be obfuscated by lack of confidence and the desire not to offend.

One of the obvious ways of tapping the true feelings and perceptions of employees is the attitude survey. A few companies have experimented widely with them, such as Shell, some of whose overseas subsidiaries have incorporated them into the routine management procedures as a regular exercise. The advantage of doing this is that the company can compare results from one year to the next. In which major areas do employees in general consider the company to be falling down? And which individual units appear to have special problems?

Don't fall into the trap of ignoring sharp criticism from 'biased' sources, such as the trade unions. There are, after all, degrees of bias, and the vehemence of the union's verbal and written assault on top management varies considerably between companies that have to deal with the same union officials. What is it that gives some chief executives better standing with their unions than others?

One of the key differences is that those with a relatively good relationship with their unions are prepared to listen to what the union has to say and to make genuine efforts to see the alternative point of view. The union leaders also accept that, in spite of differences of opinion, they are dealing with someone whose word can be relied upon, who has the authority to make decisions stick within his company. Almost invariably, the union officials equate the company with the person at the head of it; a change of chief executive can mean a swift re-evaluation by the union of its opinion of the company as a whole.

Hence it pays for those chief executives of companies who have to deal with trade unions to ensure that they do so in much the same manner as they would towards, for example, a senior partner in their merchant bank or a key supplier. You may never get the trade union entirely on your side. But just because it is not entirely with you does not mean it is against you – any more than your merchant bank might be if it does not agree with some aspect of company policy. Positive or negative, the union official's opinions of the organization and its top management will have a significant influence on the attitudes of ordinary employees. You owe it to the company to make that influence as beneficial as possible.

Another method is to create genuinely independent and anonymous systems for employees to air their concerns. One Canadian company does this through a special enquiry department forming part of the personnel department. Any employee with a problem can write it on a two-part form. One part, with the employee's name on it, is retained in a locked file that not even the chief executive has access to. The other goes to the most suitable executive to answer the query. His answer is then communicated to the employee via the enquiry department. Where a personal discussion would be helpful, the enquiry department will ask the employee if he is willing to discard his anonymity; that, however, is his decision and no pressure is exerted on him to do so.

In an era where the traditional work ethic is being replaced by a variety of more humanistic ethics, it is plain wishful thinking to expect that every employee will be devoted, committed and prepared to work long hours without complaint. But it is realistic to aim to establish that degree of involvement in a reasonably high proportion of employees – if, that is, you are prepared to do all that is necessary to promote trust, respect, understanding and competence.

What the individual manager can do   One question every manager can ask himself from time to time is 'If I believe I am strongly committed to my job and my company, how can I make sure the people below me share that enthusiasm?' Or, to put it another way, 'What kicks am I getting from my job that make this a special place to work, and how can I give my subordinates a similar sense of personal fulfilment?'

In every company there are a few managers who seem to extract a great deal more from their immediate subordinates than their peers do. Some of the things that these managers do we shall discuss later in this chapter. But, as a general observation, it is quite clear that they share the same qualities as the successful companies share. Their subordinates trust and respect them (even if they do not always like them). They in turn demonstrate a real understanding of their subordinates' work-related problems, and they are manifestly competent at the tasks those subordinates expect them to do well, such as planning and organizing.

How can you, as an individual, gain those characteristics? For a start, to be trusted and respected you must be trustworthy and respectable. Answer honestly the following questions:

● when the manager of another department complains publicly about a mistake by one of my subordinates, do I add to the coals, or do I stand up for the employee and roast him privately afterwards?

● how many times have I concealed information from or given misleading information to my subordinates in the past year?

● when my department is praised from above, do I take the credit, or do I make sure that the credit goes to the individual employees responsible?

● how often have I broken my promises to subordinates in the past year?

If you have the courage, you may find it interesting to ask your subordinates to give their own (anonymous) answers, perhaps via an intermediary in the personnel department.

The point here is that you have to work at being trusted and respected. It means having very clear standards of behaviour and sticking to them. The moment you break your own rules, you have forfeited a significant element in the effectiveness of your leadership.

The issues of understanding and competence are closely linked, both with respect and with each other. The old tradition of appointing the most skilled craftsman as the supervisor is not without merit, because such people know what the job entails and are as good at it as (if not better than) anyone working beneath them. Most people automatically respect someone who is manifestly more skilled at their own job. It is one reason why the Japanese put such heavy emphasis on starting graduates on shopfloor assembly-line work: all the employees know that all their managers have done their job themselves.

That doesn't help the British manager put in charge of a group of employees doing a specialized job he cannot – for example, the accounts functionary managing a team of data-processing specialists. Nonetheless, he can do a great deal by taking the time to gain as broad a knowledge as possible of what their jobs entail, where the major difficulties lie and what special expertise they need to produce the goods consistently and well. You don't have to be able to do their job. But you should be able to discuss their job with them in a manner that leaves them in no doubt that you are conversant with at least the fundamentals of what they are doing. It is not so much that this in itself will motivate other people; it is rather that failing to register an understanding of their jobs is likely to be taken as an admission of lack of interest, or as a sign that you do not really consider what they are doing to be important.

As an ordinary manager you have one major advantage over the chief executive in this area, because you can give very direct example by your own behaviour. Your subordinates are never likely to work alongside the chief executive; but they do work alongside you. If you arrive for work early and stay late, they will see. If you show real enthusiasm for what you are doing, you can communicate it rapidly and easily. You simply have to tell people directly and personally why it is important that this order goes out today, or that project is completed next week. Your enthusiasm will rub off, if your subordinates know you and trust you enough to accept that you are telling the truth.

PRIDE IN OWNERSHIP

What the chief executive can do   In *The Winning Streak* we found that successful companies did by and large manage to create a feeling among employees that there was something special about their employer, that there was status in working for that company, rather than for one down the road. We called that feeling 'pride in ownership' because the employees seemed to feel a proprietorial sense towards the company – a 'we' rather than 'them and us' atmosphere prevailed. While these companies tended to be leaders in extending actual ownership to employees in the form of shares, this was usually significant only in that their employees generally hung on to their shares. The share certificate seemed to become a small symbol of how they felt about their employer, so selling it in any other circumstance than financial necessity was somehow 'not quite right'.

As a symbol of the company's determination to create pride in ownership, employee share schemes are becoming more attractive and easier to administer as successive chancellors have sought methods to extend share ownership. If your company is quoted on the Stock Exchange or Unlisted Securities Market and does not have an employee share scheme, it is probably merely paying lip service to employee involvement. If the company does have a scheme, it can be a useful barometer of general attitudes towards the organization. Although there will be occasions when there are peaks of cashing in, for specific financial reasons (such as paying for summer holidays), employees who feel good about their company will generally hang on to their shares. A significant trend to sell may indicate a growth of dissatisfaction within the employees' ranks.

More important than ownership in the physical sense, however, is the way in which successful companies make people feel their jobs are useful and important – and hence by inference that *they* are useful and important. This they do partly by ensuring that the company is seen to be providing a valuable service to its customers and the community, and partly by making every job count.

Among ways in which you can emulate that process are:

● make the company one they can be proud to work for. Take an objective look from outside the company and ask yourself 'What is there about this organization that I feel proud of?' Make a list of all the points you can feel proud of and all those you can't. Of the ones you can feel proud of, ask yourself 'Are we doing enough to tell people about these things?' Most companies are far less adept at selling their virtues to the employees than they are at selling their virtues to their customers. Look at your company's employee newspaper, for example. How often are the points you feel proud of the company for mentioned in it? You can open employees' eyes to the good things about their company in a wide range of ways, with a little imagination. For example, why not ask in some of your best customers from time to time, to tell employees what they think about your company and the way it does business? Perhaps you can share with the employees your list of things to be proud of – indeed, why not? As regards those points you have listed as not feeling proud of, some remedial action may well be needed. You can, of course, establish new policies, allocate resources and generally provide support in each of these areas – indeed, that is a large part of the chief executive's job. But the greatest gains may come from openly admitting to the employees where the company's weaknesses lie, and involving them in seeking and implementing the remedies.

- establish the brand name. Whether your company is in the consumer or the industrial field, employees who know they produce a good product get a special feeling of pride when they see one of 'theirs' on the shop shelf or in use. The presence of a strong brand name is a signal that the product matters. If that brand name and the company name are closely associated on the packaging, in the advertising and elsewhere (e.g. Kellogg's Corn Flakes or Cadbury's Dairy Milk) the internal impact is even stronger, simply because it tells everyone that the company values the product enough to insist that everybody knows who it is made by. One of the most common mistakes made by companies in pushing their brand names is to emphasize that they are the biggest in the market, or among the cheapest in their range. This may be all very well for the short term, but as a long-term tactic it has dangerous flaws. For a start, these are attributes that may easily be lost, in which case the brand ends up with no identity at all. Secondly, they are not attributes that motivate employees, and there is also some doubt as to how effective they are in customer relations. The brand attributes that count in motivating employees are consistent high quality and public acceptance that they are 'good' products made by a reliable company. Producing a commodity, however useful it may be, has no social status. Producing a known and valued brand does. Listen to yourself and to your spouse at a party. When someone asks you what you do, do you reply, for example, 'I'm chairman of a plastics company', or do you say 'I'm chairman of Dreadnought PLC'. Ask some of your more junior employees what they say. If they are honest with you, you may gain a useful insight into the value and perception of your brands.

● pay more than lip service to participation. The campaigns conducted by the strange alliance of employers' organizations, left-wing trade unions and the Government against the European Commission's conception of industrial democracy all reflect a feeling that you cannot legislate for good human relations. Yet few of the up-and-coming generation of top managers would deny that there are substantial payoffs to the company that can involve its ordinary employees in resolving difficult problems. Those, for example, that have opened the books to employee representatives, and involved them closely in decisions on how manpower reductions should be carried out, have by and large had a smoother ride in industrial relations during the recent recession than those that have relied upon managerial prerogative.

Giving people a say in the decisions that affect their jobs and their future can be a stabilizing influence, not least because it increases their general sense of security. It has, however, taken twenty years and more for Swedish companies to become adjusted to regular consultation with employees and to persuade employees to use the participation process in an initiatory rather than a reactive manner – and few Swedish companies would admit to being fully satisfied with the working of their participation schemes even now. So it is unrealistic to expect that an executive decision to become more participative is going to change much in the short term. Just as a marketing effort needs to be sustained and constantly reinforced to create high awareness and consumer acceptance, so it takes a long time to turn an autocratic company culture into a democratic one. Some managers may prove incapable of operating in a participative manner. Even if those managers were to be removed and replaced by dynamic organizers with a passionate belief in the virtues of participation, ordinary employees who have spent most of their working lives being told what to do and never being asked for their opinion may find the transition equally hard.

In spite of the difficulties, if you aim to use the resources of your company to their fullest effect, you will have to ensure that some degree of employee participation takes place. The first decision to make is how far you are prepared to go. Do you want to consult with employees – i.e. inform and listen but retain executive power – or introduce co-determination, where you share power? In the more likely situation that you wish to consult employees, for example, do you want to consult about...?

- shopfloor issues
- domestic investment and disinvestment decisions
- international investment and disinvestment decisions – already a reality in a handful of countries)
- hire and fire decisions – in some companies in Continental Europe, employees are closely involved in choosing new recruits, in handling disciplinary matters, and in one or two cases in the selection of their immediate superior

Do you want to consult employees via relatively informal structures, such as semi-autonomous work groups on the shopfloor, or do you want to install a formal participation structure, perhaps with worker directors and all the other trappings that go with involving employee representatives in the power structure of the company? In the latter case, do you understand and have you fully considered the implications of having unqualified people on the board?

If you take the informal route to participation, it probably doesn't matter a great deal how you organize it, as long as everyone in the organization understands what the objectives are and why this particular route has been taken, and as long as top management's commitment to participation is deep and permanent. Once you start the process, you can go back only at hefty cost in management–employee relations. One of the discoveries by the Swedish Employers' Federation was that the participation schemes that worked were those that became firmly embedded into the routine ways of doing things within the organization, and were consistent with the company culture. Those that were grafted on as a kind of external skeleton rarely resulted in significant changes of attitude and behaviour by either management or the trade unions.

It used to be thought that participation could not be imposed from above. In reality, it will only work if top management takes a clear lead, outlining exactly what it hopes to achieve and why. One common feature of many successful participation schemes is that they only really start working when top management asks the employees to help in a crisis. Such was the case, for example, at telecommunications company TRW-Carr. In the early 1980s, the company was going through a traumatic upheaval, with five factories being consolidated into two, manpower being cut from 1,000 to 450 people and over £1 million being invested into new machinery.

Chief Executive magazine reported that top management recognized that the lip service they had paid to employee participation had not always been followed through. So, as productivity problems arose, they resolved to seek ways to involve the employees in solving them. One long-standing issue was an employee grievance over pay differentials on the shopfloor. This was resolved by training a job evaluation team, in which the employees outnumbered the managers, and giving this team responsibility for finding fair solutions. Another problem arose in a new production team, which had taken over connector assembly work transferred from another plant. Quality had fallen dramatically, with rejects running at 10 per cent, and the quantity of scrap was very high. Managing director Derek Tomlins asked the operators to sort it out for themselves, in a discussion group. The reject rate fell immediately to 6 per cent, and within twelve weeks to 1 per cent – considerably better than in the old plant.

To these *ad hoc* solutions was added a formal programme of sensing sessions. Tomlins explains:

> We choose 12 people at random, and take them off site, to somewhere they can sit down comfortably. I let them ask me any questions they wish. We make notes and circulate them in the factory later as anonymous questions and answers. They have brought up personality problems we did not know about which were hindering productivity. They have made suggestions on improving throughout. One person recently asked, 'Why did we send four separate shipments to the same customer within ten days?' They highlighted a lot of production problems.

What such examples illustrate is that a great deal more can be achieved by getting the employees to work with you than for you.

It is also essential to make genuine efforts to ensure that every job is interesting and worthwhile. It may not be possible to achieve, but there are a great many laurels to be gained just for trying. On the shopfloor and in the office, new technology gives you two choices – creating monotonous, repetitive jobs dealing with only one part of a process or creating varied, more rewarding jobs. Most boring jobs are created by default rather than design. What is needed to avoid creating them is, first, a positive commitment to organizing the available work and the capital investment so that humanizing work and providing challenge are built-in objectives rather than last-minute add-ons; and second, an acceptance that any additional costs of creating interesting jobs will be more than repaid in terms of higher quality of work, if not in higher volume of production.

What the individual manager can do   You can't normally do much on your own about the overall reputation of the company or the status of its brand name. You can, however, do a lot for the reputation of your department within the company as a whole, with the aim of increasing the sense of pride your subordinates feel about working under your leadership.

Among simple things you can do are:

- give subordinates copies of any memos you send to more senior management praising an achievement by someone in your department, or memos of praise to you from above. Don't be afraid to ask senior managers to pen a few lines from time to time.
- explain to your subordinates how what they do helps other departments. Give 'Brownie points' to people who go out of their way to be helpful to other departments.
- seek assignments for your department that will have high visibility throughout the company
- volunteer your department as the guinea pig for new ideas. Most people like to feel they are leading change rather than being led by change.
- even if your company does not have a participative culture, you can create one in your area of responsibility. It is a strange hangover from the early years of this century that many British managers are so preoccupied with their role as the giver of orders that they find it hard, even impossible, to ask subordinates for help. But here is a transformation that must come about, because tomorrow's effective manager is essentially a teamworker, a leader from within, rather than an autocrat. If you genuinely see your department as a team, and yourself as the engine that

drives it, it is relatively easy to pull everyone else along with you when you up your own revs.

● never be afraid to share your problems with subordinates. Even if your relationship with a subordinate is so poor that you are afraid he might use the situation against you, by going to more senior management, it is a wise move – under the circumstances, any such behaviour on his part will automatically be seen by your superiors and peers as disloyalty. Indeed, by sharing problems in this way, many besieged managers have turned hostile subordinates into their fiercest supporters. It is not unusual for a manager to have a problem to resolve, and there is no shame in it – indeed without problems, who would need managers in the first place? Keeping problems to yourself usually only makes them grow.

● within the limits of your responsibility, try to arrange jobs to give variety, interest and above all challenge to your subordinates. You will normally have far more influence over this process than senior management ever can, because you can directly observe what makes up individual jobs and what each person is good at. By sharing your objectives, you can involve them in your challenges, to the extent that they will ask to take on specific tasks and responsibilities.

The content of most jobs is based on historical events, with minor additions or deletions as new equipment or requirements are introduced. Rarely, if ever, does the job content receive a total overhaul. Yet, if your job as a manager includes making the most efficient use of the human resources under your control, the matching of people and tasks should be a matter for regular review. So, from time to time, involve the employees in your department in dissecting all the tasks that need to be done and in deciding how they should be parcelled out. You will almost certainly discover ambitions you knew nothing of: for example, the typist who wants to learn about basic book-keeping, or the machine operator who would like to take responsibility for the electrical maintenance of his equipment. In this way, you may be able to change routine jobs into the kind of jobs that ordinary people can actually look forward to in the mornings.

Of course, all these activities are likely to benefit you in personal career terms, too, by bringing your performance and that of your unit frequently to top management's notice.

HIGH DEGREE OF COMMUNICATIONS

What the chief executive can do   Considering that this is the era of advanced communications, it is amazing how ineffective many companies' internal communications are. The reasons for this failure seem to lie primarily in a lack of objectives regarding communications rather than in any desire not to communicate.

A few – very few – companies conduct communications audits, which provide a certain amount of information on who is communicating what to whom. But the process really needs to start from the top, with the chief executive establishing whom he needs to communicate with and why. The next step is to let those people in on the secret, too. We have seen numerous communications disasters where chief executives have been persuaded that they should communicate more, and have rushed into print or video with little or no idea of what they aimed to accomplish. Not surprisingly, the employees don't have much idea either, and frequently assume it is just another ill-considered public relations exercise – which, to be fair, is often quite accurate. For an internal company communications programme to be effective, everyone concerned must appreciate what the point of the exercise is.

This basic piece of common sense provides the reason for the dismal failure of many cascade briefing programmes, where top management briefs middle management, middle management briefs junior management and so on down to the lowest levels. Briefing meetings are all very well if you've got something to say. Unfortunately, they too often become a matter of habit, with little content, especially if the information has become progressively diluted and junior management is little wiser about the implications of the bland statements it reads out than the shopfloor audience itself. All too often briefings become no more than a copout where top management doesn't dare to face the troops and leaves it to junior management. Employees on the whole prefer to hear the message from the organ grinder, not the monkey.

Communications is such an important part of the chief executive's role that it deserves to be taken seriously. Among practical steps for the chief executive to take are:

● make use of the whole range of communications media available to you, from print to the new information technologies that can put the same message instantly on every employee's desktop terminal. Make the message consistent, keep it relatively simple and repeat it as often as possible through as many media as possible. Many British companies, for example, never think of using posters to communicate with employees, yet do not hesitate to use them to communicate with the general public. The only real difference between the internal and external audiences is that the people inside the company may have more interest.

● do remember the lessons of visible management and stomp the sites, talking to the employees in person. The most credible form of communication is still face to face, in small groups or one to one, but better talk to people *en masse* than not at all.

● always be honest in your communications. Better to say nothing than to prevaricate.

● break bad news sooner rather than later. The longer you sit on it, the worse the rumours and the greater the likelihood of a leak.

● have a clear policy on what can and cannot be passed on to the employees. In general, everything can and should be communicable, unless there is a specific written policy reason for not doing so. Don't assume that just because an item of information is commercially sensitive, you can't trust employees with it. Most people become remarkably trustworthy when they feel they are trusted. If they feel you can't trust them, then they are unlikely to trust you. Try to make sure that *all* information – including the most sensitive – is accessible to a few employees trusted by their peers, or to an external ombudsman who can provide reassurance that all is well, or at least under control.

An example of the benefits of open information is the experience of companies in the United States and West Germany in dealing with data privacy legislation. Those companies that have kept to the spirit rather than just the letter of the legislation have found that opening up records in a controlled manner has actually reduced administrative time spent on record keeping. The proportion of employees asking to see their personal files in companies with an open record policy has been far smaller than in companies without such a policy. Several companies now distribute personnel records to employees annually asking them to verify their accuracy. The first time one company in West Germany did this, it found that more than half had errors in them – which meant, in effect, that the personnel record system was dangerously unreliable. Open information now ensures that it is virtually 100 per cent accurate.

Ask yourself 'How sure am I that the information we hold in our company is generally accurate? How much more accurate would it be if more people had access to it? Is there really any tenable reason why they shouldn't have access to it?' In most cases, the only reasons information is withheld from people in the company are habit and the reluctance of managers to share information, because information is power.

To be more accurate, information *was* power. You as chief executive now have the ability to break the connection between information and raw power by making intelligent use of information technology. Until recently, information systems churned out data for individual departments. The managers of those departments could hoard their data, parcelling it out as they saw advantage in so doing, or grudgingly as they were pressured from elsewhere. Now, however, modern management information systems are open to anyone with the correct access code. You have to make a decision whether to allow managers to lock away their data under computer key or to insist that data is pooled for access by everyone with a good reason. Many managers may see this latter course as a personal threat. Not only does it undermine their power base, but it makes their performance far more transparent than has ever been the case before. While that may be bad for the individual, for the organization as a whole it must be a healthy and invigorating process.

Don't forget that effective communications is three-way – down, up and lateral. Most of the media you use to talk down can also be used to talk up and across the organization. Actively encourage employees to write letters to you and make sure you at least sign the replies. Few employees will ever think to write to you unless you make it clear you are happy for them to do so. Among those letters will be the clues to serious problems, a smattering of potentially valuable ideas and a great deal of steam being safely let off.

Another medium less well used than it might be is the company newspaper. Usually very cheaply and badly produced, it carries a clear visual message of indifference when placed next door to the glossy sales literature in the company foyer. It says, 'Customers are valued more than employees.' The content is usually superficial and one-way. Employee attitudes and comments tend to be limited to approved articles on sales drives, sports and competitions. Yet the employee newspaper is a superb vehicle for signed or anonymous constructive criticism of company policy. It will, however, only be used as such if employees observe that the contents do not always follow the party line and that dissent is actually encouraged within its pages. Of course, to do this does take the courage of confident leadership.

Have an 'open door' policy, and make sure you welcome anyone who uses it. It is no use announcing that your door is always open if you are not really prepared to listen to the people who come through it. The CEO of a US airline was taken aback one busy morning, when a pilot arrived in his antechamber and demanded an audience. 'What's the problem?' asked the CEO. 'No problem,' said the pilot, 'I just wanted to see if you meant what you said about having an open door.' That chief executive didn't bawl the pilot out. Far from it. He made sure the story went the rounds of the grapevine, because he recognized what an excellent advertisement it was for the open management approach.

What the individual manager can do Virtually all the advice to the chief executive applies equally to you. The more information you share with your subordinates, the more you oblige them to become colleagues rather than underlings. Always be honest with them; trust them with information unless you have a really strong reason for not doing so, and tell them both good news and bad news as soon as you can. Unlike the chief executive, you can sit down with them and explain in as much detail as they need the background to the information you give them – which means that you may sometimes find yourself sent off to gather information you do not have. Don't resent that: a growing part of the modern manager's role is to facilitate the provision of information, not to act as its filter.

Don't forget, either, that you have a role in communicating employees' concerns upwards. One of the loudest complaints of chief executives in heavily unionized industries is that they often hear of problems from the union officials before they hear of them through their own channels. To some extent this is because the company information channels have more layers to go through. But it is also because intervening layers of management use their own judgement on what information they believe top management will want to hear. You, as the leader of your team, must insist that issues that concern your subordinates are not spiked halfway up the management hierarchy, but receive a swift and adequate response.

HIGH PAY AND/OR INCENTIVES

What the chief executive can do   Do most people in your company say they are underpaid, or paid about right, or overpaid? If you have a 20:70:10 ratio, you are probably about right. The 20 per cent who feel they are underpaid probably are not really earning what they are paid now and simply have an exaggerated expectation of their own worth. The 10 per cent who feel they are overpaid may be right, but these should be the people you most want to retain in the organization.

Look at the issue of pay less in terms of market value (though that is important) than how much the person is worth to your company. Is it important for you to keep them?

Recent surveys suggest that British managers are among the lowest paid in the developed nations. The argument that internationally competitive remuneration will make the company as a whole less competitive has always sounded a little hollow. Is the more correct correlation perhaps that the less you value people, the less they have to live up to? Would British managers be more productive if more were invested in them, in terms of salary, supporting facilities and training? The experience of successful companies says yes. The lesson is clear.

Of course, there are other components of the compensation package than salary alone. Executive incentive schemes, according to a recent survey by Inbucon Management Consultants, are now gaining rapidly in popularity. Of 248 companies surveyed, 160 had incentive schemes and a third of the remainder planned to introduce them within twelve months. Some 95 per cent of those companies with schemes reported them to be at least partly living up to expectations. Where they appear to fall down, however, is as a means of improving the retention of key staff.

It is vital to ensure that the incentives not only work hand in hand with, but positively drive the achievement of, objectives. Incentives should be incremental, and not merely supplement an inadequate basic pay level. In addition, they should be determined by a balanced combination of company, unit and individual performance assessed over the short, medium and long term.

What the individual manager can do   You can't have much effect on salary or incentive policy. But you can do a great deal to create an environment in which your subordinates can make the most of the incentive opportunities available. Work out with them how you can help them earn more while the company earns more. If your own earnings are partially or wholly tied to how well they perform, you benefit, too.

PROMOTION FROM WITHIN

What the chief executive can do   In *The Winning Streak* we found that both successful and unsuccessful companies promoted from within, but that the successful companies pushed people into general management positions much earlier. You, as chief executive, have to ensure that people with high potential are not allowed to become trapped in one narrow function. While not every job is suitable for rotation, every individual may be. Just because someone is an accountant, that does not mean that he cannot learn a great deal from a spell in sales or personnel. The wider a person's experience at a relatively early age, the easier it will be to find successive niches for him as he climbs the promotional ladder. Waiting to fill dead men's shoes is soul-destroying for the frustrated employee, and a recipe for low productivity for the company. Part of the personnel policy should be an automatic evaluation of what has gone wrong when someone remains in the same job for more than five years.

While you do not want to starve the organization of new blood, most senior appointments should be able to be made from inside. The only circumstances in which a high proportion of outside appointments is justified are where you are trying to make a rapid and sweeping change of culture that requires managers with completely different ways of thinking. If, under any other circumstances, you discover that more than 25 per cent of senior appointments are coming from outside, you should investigate closely what is so wrong with the internal training and manpower planning processes that they miss so many key requirements.

What the individual manager can do   The greatest block to many managers' promotion or job rotation is the lack of a suitable successor or regent. You can improve promotion chances for both yourself and your subordinates by developing their potential. From time to time delegate to them parts of your job that will increase their knowledge and ability. Let them stand in for you at meetings. Pinpoint training needs, and make sure the people receive the training you recommend. When they can almost fill your shoes, you will most likely need and merit a bigger pair.

TRAINING

What the chief executive can do There are certain steps which only the chief executive can take. The first of these is to ensure that the training operation is accorded adequate status in the company. It must not be a repository for embarrassing has-beens, but a department where high-flying young managers are frequently seconded to gain valuable experience. The second is to ensure that training receives adequate funding. Next to advertising and public relations, training is the most easily and frequently pruned activity in times of cost cutting.

By comparison with our international rivals, British firms spend depressingly little on training their employees, according to research by the Institute of Manpower Studies. It is, therefore, hardly surprising that key sectors, such as information technology, are facing an appalling 'skills gap'. The principal cause of this gap is that most companies prefer to poach trained people rather than grow their own.

Because your view as chief executive of a company bent on winning is a long-term view, you will want to put pressure on your personnel department to find ways both to train the people you will need in the future and to keep them with you once their training is completed. You will, of course, continue to lose a proportion of the people you train. But you will benefit by attracting people of higher quality in the first place.

It will be expensive; that cannot be denied. But new, more cost-effective training methods and technologies are emerging all the time. A great deal, for example, can be accomplished at low cost by providing employees with the facilities to teach themselves. You must put constant pressure on the training department to make every training pound count. Even if the cost is high, remember that better trained, more qualified employees generally produce greater added value.

Investment in training is an essential part of international competition. Try to find out what your international competitors spend per head on training. Equal it, plus a bit more to make up for the deficiencies of previous years. Make it a goal to have a better trained workforce than they do, and you will end up with a better workforce than they have.

What the individual manager can do   Training budgets may be out of your hands, but you can ensure that everyone under your supervision receives at least some training over the course of each year. Talk with them about what they do well or badly in their current jobs and about what they need to learn for the next job they would like to do. Remember that, in the end, training is still a line responsibility. The employees may go on courses run by the training department, or receive advice on specific training needs, but you are responsible for directing their development. Rather than leave their training to an overstretched and frequently under-resourced training department, you must make opportunities for them to learn on the job.

THE SOCIAL SIDE OF WORK

What the chief executive can do   Work can be both serious and fun at the same time. How many people do you know, for example, who are deadly serious about their hobbies? You can make the frustrations that occur in any job a small part of the price for work people enjoy in several ways:

- establish a clear policy that the company actively wants to enrich everyone's job, that it does want people to enjoy their work. Provide resources for any form of job enrichment that will pay for itself in increased productivity within a reasonable period of time, and encourage managers to create viable job enrichment programmes within their operations.

- give managers the budgetary freedom to let their hair down with subordinates from time to time when the department has made a major achievement or when everyone has made exceptional efforts to help the company. Don't allow such celebrations as a matter of routine, but as a specific reward for a specific effort. If you were to hide a tape recorder at the typical office Christmas party (and we hasten to add we are not in the least suggesting that you should), you might find a fairly high degree of cynicism towards the company and its motives, which would be quite absent when people can relate the event to their own personal efforts.

What the individual manager can do Look for specific ways in which your subordinates' jobs could be enriched, and ask them for their suggestions. You may well find they are not used to this kind of consideration from an employer, and you may have to persevere to convince them that they can influence their work content and environment. If job enrichment means special training or new equipment, you must, of course, make out the case for the expenditure in terms of the financial returns to the company. But don't be slow in making out the human resource case, too. The phrase 'The expenditure would have a beneficial effect upon the morale of this employee' can carry additional weight, especially in a company concerned to raise productivity through employee motivation.

You don't have to go off to the pub with your subordinates every evening to convince them that you are happy to socialize with them. But you should make yourself available to talk with them in a more relaxed environment outside the office or plant. Socializing can break down barriers. But it has to be genuine, a natural outcome of working as a team. You simply cannot expect to gain trust and confidence in this way if you are 'the boss' inside the company premises and 'genial old Harry' outside. All that will earn you is a reputation for being two-faced. Socializing out of office hours needs to be an extension of the informal team atmosphere that exists during work hours, or else it creates an invidious comparison that may actually harm your relationships with subordinates.

GENUINE RESPECT FOR THE INDIVIDUAL

What the chief executive can do At one time during the 1970s, every other company chairman was including in his annual report or luncheon speeches the claim that 'People are our greatest asset.' When asked how much they were spending on maintaining, developing and generally looking after that asset, most would prevaricate, become embarrassed and try to change the subject. Then came the recession, when they had to lay off thousands of employees, and the phrase disappeared rapidly from the vocabulary of most top managers.

It is, however, still as true as it ever was. Apart from a few exceptional cases, winning companies win not because of their financial or physical resources but because of the quality, commitment and creativity of the people who make up the organization. Anything that reduces the effectiveness of those people reduces the effectiveness of the whole organization. Therefore ask yourself 'How much do the people in this organization really matter to me? What responsibilities do we, or should we, have towards them?'

If you want the company to matter to the employees, if you want them to care what happens to the company and its customers, then they have to feel sure that the company genuinely cares about them. The strong welfare orientation of companies such as Marks & Spencer or the John Lewis Partnership has its origins in an era when desperate poverty was a fact of life for millions of people in Britain and when State support for the poor hardly existed. That does not mean, however, that it is now irrelevant. The entire personal insurance industry exists on people's desire to add a degree of security to their lives, to know that personal crises can be prevented from becoming catastrophes. The caring company provides that same kind of reassurance.

One of the most interesting employee welfare schemes introduced to Britain in recent years is Control Data's Employee Advisory Resource. EAR is a twenty-four-hour-a-day confidential counselling service used by the company's 3000 British staff. A team of three counsellors is available to talk to employees at any hour, in person or by telephone. Counsellors visit each of the company plants regularly and there is always someone available via a paging system.

In its first six months, EAR dealt with a flood of employee problems, including how to apply for UK citizenship, how to trace a missing person, how to find a childminder, get a mortgage, or cope with a divorce, how to return defective goods to a manufacturer, and crisis intervention in suicide, drugs and alcoholism. When employees were polled to determine their attitudes on this service, the response was almost entirely positive. EAR advertises itself and announces the next visit by a counsellor on all the company notice boards, stressing that its services are completely confidential. This confidentiality is maintained by keeping the counsellor out of the obvious departments such as personnel or welfare; EAR reports only to the chief executive.

People who are unwilling to talk to their immediate superior, their friends or their family usually show much less reluctance to discuss matters with a neutral third party.

In the main, the help EAR gives is a sympathetic ear, coupled with advice on where to go to obtain the specific additional help the employee needs. If the problem is a work matter, counsellors try to solve it through the existing machinery, although they can only do so with the employee's agreement. If there is a gap in the machinery, counsellors can involve the authority of the chief executive in taking steps to fill it.

Although it is not possible to put clear money values on the savings from the EAR programme, the senior counsellor says, 'There's no doubt that home and work have a real effect on each other. Your worries don't just stop when you walk into the office or through the factory gate. People can solve almost all of these worries themselves, but they have to know where to start.'

No matter how much effort the company puts into caring for its employees, there will, none the less, always be the possibility that it will have to make some of them redundant. In human asset terms, this is the equivalent of writing off an investment and should always be regarded as a failure, even when the employees involved have simply been made obsolete by automation. You have to ask 'Could better strategic planning and new product development have provided alternative work for these people? Could you have started retraining them a year or more ago to equip them for jobs in other parts of the business?' If you could have, why didn't you?

If employees must go, then top management should not be afraid to take the blame. Mealy-mouthed excuses about international trading conditions or the value of the dollar cannot disguise the fact that either you didn't predict a change in the company's operating environment, or you failed to plan what to do with human assets you knew would be released.

Once you have admitted your responsibility to yourself, it becomes much easier to understand the need to deal with the dispossessed employees in a fair and generous manner: 'Our mistake. What can we do to help?' A whole variety of options then opens up to ease the transition of these employees into alternative employment or into an early retirement they will willingly accept.

What the individual manager can do   Be honest: how much respect do you have for the people who work for you? If it is less than it might be, how much of that gap could possibly be your fault?

Respect has to be mutual to be productive. The more you show that you respect your subordinates for what they can do well, by timely words of praise, the more they will respond and seek to become more worthy of respect. If they have weaknesses, it is part of your job to help them overcome those weaknesses. In other words, you must take each individual in your department and develop him or her until you can respect them all at the very least for their competence, if not for their personality. You may also find that you receive a great deal more respect from them.

You have a welfare role, too, for anything that affects productivity in your department is your problem. The Control Data programme we referred to earlier was started because the company found that the most frequent absentees were not malingerers, but people who were normally among the most conscientious of employees, with good work records. The one thing they all had in common was that they all had personal problems at the time. You can keep a weather eye open for signs of personal stress and maintain a genuine open door for employees with a personal problem – especially where an employee's work performance is tailing off. You may not be able to help in any practical way, and you should not become embroiled in resolving problems outside the workplace. But you can refer the employee to sources of help and make it clear that you and the company are giving support in a difficult time. In general, the employee whose company sticks by him sticks by his company.

Trust, respect, understanding and competence: you can develop them in most of the people in your organization. But first, whether you are chief executive, shopfloor supervisor or anywhere between, you must demonstrate them yourself.

5 Winning through market orientation

One of the clearest differences that *The Winning Streak* showed between successful and unsuccessful companies was in their attitude towards their markets. The unsuccessful companies lived in their markets; the successful ones lived their markets. If you wish to develop the winning streak in your marketing, you must absorb the market and its requirements into the pores of your organization; the company and the market must become as one. That requires a high degree of sensitivity and reaction to market change and an instinct for how to direct it rather than simply be swept along with it. The following questions draw on some of the experiences of 'winning streak' companies that have learnt this lesson.

GENERAL QUESTIONS

1 Does the board of your company genuinely understand the difference between sales and marketing?

2 In your company is ...?

> *sales subordinate to marketing*
> *sales equal in status to marketing*
> *marketing subordinate to sales*

3 In your company is marketing ...?

> *consulted or involved in every other major department's activity*
> *consulted or involved in some major departments' activities*
> *obliged to mind its own business*

4a Does top management establish clear objectives for the marketing plan, based on and in harmony with the overall corporate objectives?

b At what stage of the budgeting process is the marketing plan drafted?

> *at the end*
> *at the beginning*
> *as the other plans become clear*

5 Is marketing seen as an activity which should involve ...?

> *all senior managers*
> *some senior managers*
> *only the marketing manager/director*

6 A new product flops because people don't like some of its characteristics. Would this normally be seen as ...?

> *a problem for marketing, sales and production together*
> *a marketing problem*
> *a sales problem*
> *a production problem*
> *anybody's problem as long as its not mine*

BRAND STRENGTH

7 Does market research show that people regard your company as different from its competitors?

8 Are your main brands ...?

> *better regarded than the competition*
> *equally regarded with the competition*
> *less well regarded than the competition*
> *don't know*

9 Have any major products from your company become 'commoditized' in recent years? (e.g. airline seats, most mueslis and most beers are now bought without regard to who supplies them – in spite of the brand name, people treat the product or service as a commodity.)

10 Is spending on brand planning ...?

a consistent, planned operation spanning at least five years
a spasmodic injection of advertising according to an annual plan
little and not very often

11 How important is the achievement of market leadership to your company?

very: it's central to our philosophy – we'll buy market share if we have to
moderately: we would rather be the most consistently profitable company than the one with the most volume
moderately: we rarely have the resources to seize or hold market leadership – we don't like to become targets
unimportant

CUSTOMER RELATIONS

12 Have senior managers in your company ever posed as a customer with a complaint to test the complaints-handling system (or hired an outside agency to do the same task)?

13 Does top management see copies of or analyse customers' complaints ...?

frequently
occasionally
rarely or never

14 What is the status of the manager directly responsible for customer relations? (i.e. who signs the replies to serious complaints?)

board level
senior management
middle management
junior management
no such function in our firm

15   How swiftly does your company acknowledge written or telephone complaints?

> *within twenty-four hours*
> *within forty-eight hours*
> *within a week*
> *within a month*
> *we don't bother to respond at all*

16   How closely are patterns of complaints analysed?

> *very*
> *moderately*
> *not at all*

17   How often does top management personally contact aggrieved customers?

> *for any serious complaint*
> *for some serious complaints*
> *never*

QUALITY CONTROL

18   How closely can you identify the source of each problem that leads to a complaint about some of your products?

> *to the individual employee*
> *to the individual department*
> *to the plant*
> *not at all*

19   What percentage of staff would you estimate espouse the quality ethic in your company?

> *all*
> *more than half*
> *less than half*

20   How involved does your company become in the quality control methods of its suppliers?

closely
a little
not at all

21 Which of the following best describes your company's approach to quality control?

get it right first time: quality begins and ends with the operator and his equipment
test and check by sample
if it's not right, the customer will soon tell us

22 Does your company openly value product quality as an employee motivator?

HUNGER FOR MARKET INFORMATION

23 Is market research in your company ...?

allocated a formal budget
updated regularly
rarely used

24 Do you know your competitors' strengths and weaknesses ...?

better than they know themselves
pretty well
moderately well
hardly at all
not even sure who they are

25 How closely are sales, production and advertising activity tied to research data?

completely
partially
hardly at all

MARKET-ORIENTED R&D

26   In developing new products and processes does your company . . . ?

form inter-disciplinary teams, with finance and marketing strongly represented
make R&D produce what marketing or sales says it needs
let R&D produce what it thinks marketing or sales should be selling

27   Does your company send R&D people into the field to gain the customer's viewpoint?

ACTION-ORIENTED MARKETING

28   What level of contingency planning does the marketing department make?

high: we want to cover any likely eventuality
moderate: we have contingency plans, but it takes a while to bring them on stream
low: we make a plan and stick to it
low: we make a plan and change it to fit the circumstances as they happen

---

POINTS TO WATCH:

Question 2: this issue is a minefield. In theory, as we shall see on page 114, sales should be subordinate to marketing. In practice, the relationship may depend on the calibre of person and the role of marketing. If marketing's primary function is simply to pump out statistics and sales-support literature, it can be disastrous to place it in charge of sales. If top management wishes marketing to assume its proper strategic function, however, it must give marketing some measure of responsibility for directing where and how sales efforts are applied. It must also ensure that the person in the marketing hot seat has the capability to perform that demanding role. One of the key attributes is team-building ability.

Question 11: another tricky one. While much of the research into competitive advantage suggests that market leaders are usually more successful (i.e. more profitable) than market followers, it is easy to fall into the trap of chasing market leadership for its own sake. It may in many cases be more profitable in the long term to redefine the market you are in.

GENERAL POINTS

What the chief executive can do   Every effective chief executive is a marketer, no matter what business discipline he began his career in. The company's marketing strategy (or lack of it) pervades virtually every aspect of its activities. It is, indeed, the game plan upon which sales, production, manpower, distribution and supply all need to be based. However much he may delegate the operational side of marketing to a marketing director, the chief executive cannot afford to delegate the construction of marketing strategy. If he is not closely involved he is abdicating rather than delegating. He must set the objectives for and demand a viable marketing plan, and ensure that the marketing function has the resources it needs to plan effectively. This is the only way a chief executive can fully commit himself and everyone else in the company to objectives that meet market needs.

Among essential steps for the chief executive in taking control of marketing strategy are:

● really know your market and how your company fits into it. 'Of course I know our market,' you may say. But how *well* do you know it? Can you draw a diagram now that shows how the market you are in interfaces with other markets? Are you sure you understand all the potential threats to your market and all the potential opportunities to penetrate those nearby markets? How sure are you that your vision of the market is based on tomorrow rather than yesterday? Are the assumptions you make about the market based on past experience or on objective assessments and measurements made today? How often do you re-evaluate your assumptions about the market? How comfortable are you with your answers?

● really know what the market thinks of you. You may think your company is something special in the marketplace, but does the outside world? It is depressingly easy to assume that the points you value in your own company are equally valued by the marketplace. In reality the marketplace may not care a fig about the speed of your service, the breadth of your product range, or the fact that 60 per cent of the professional staff have science degrees. What counts (assuming there is a market for the product or service at all) is how the market sees your company *vis-à-vis* its competitors. The marketing tools used to create awareness of your company and its offerings are primarily a matter for the marketing functionaries to worry about. But you, as chief executive, have a responsibility to ensure that the company is capable of delivering what the market wants in a manner far superior to that of the competition. It is relatively easy to sell a positive image if you have a darned good story to tell in the first place. The only way to find out what the market thinks of you is to ask it, through regular and thorough market research.

- make the company marketing-oriented rather than sales-oriented. If your company is to be market-oriented, the marketing function has to provide the overview of which the sales effort is a part. Even in a commodity market, where the only things that appear to count are price and salesmanship, an effective marketing overview can often make a substantial difference when it comes to customer choice. Take the cement industry, for example. One bag of cement manufactured in Britain is much like another. Even the price is the same. The differences are the label on the packaging – and the customer service. It is no surprise that the cement manufacturers exert a great deal of effort to make sure that they understand customer needs and are able to deliver at short notice, with no fuss. That's marketing, not sales. Strategic marketing is not possible if marketing is simply a service department to sales, because sales is essentially a short-horizon activity.

- make sure marketing has the right to poke its nose into everyone else's business. Although department managers in production or R&D, for example, may find it annoying to have someone from outside telling them they are doing their job wrong, nobody benefits if they go merrily on their way producing something that does not fit the market need. The marketing department needs to be involved at the earliest possible stage of new product development, product changes and – all too often forgotten – any internal administrative changes that may affect the way the product is delivered to the market or supported once it gets there. The quality of wrapping paper, the automation of a warehouse, or the installation of a new telephone system, for example, are all areas where the company's interface with its market may be affected. Of course, it is far better to involve marketing in such matters by virtue of team membership rather than as an interloper. The more the company takes decisions through *ad hoc* and formal teams, the easier it is for marketing to exert its influence on other departments. Part of your job as chief executive is to ensure that such teams are formed and that they are effective. You will know that you are on the right track when all the department heads in the company are prepared to share responsibility for a failure in the marketplace and are prepared to learn from the experience together, to prevent a similar failure in future.

- insist that marketing is every manager's responsibility. Because marketing pervades all departments, all departments must take some responsibility for it. You would not, for example, expect the manager of the warehouse to authorize massive amounts of overtime without first working out the cost. So why let him ignore the potentially greater damage he may do (especially since it takes a lot longer to become evident) by ignoring the marketing implications of his decisions?

- become the marketing champion. By demonstrating your commitment to marketing thinking and by hammering home to other managers why the marketing dimension is so important in specific decisions you have made, you can encourage every manager (and through them, every employee) to think in terms of customers and markets.

- whatever you do, don't take the theories of marketing strategy too seriously. One of the principal reasons for the stagnation of many large firms in the 1970s, was that they relied too heavily upon portfolio theory and ideas of product life cycle. Apart from the fact that everyone else was using the same theories, and therefore taking the same general strategy, none of these theories provide more than a guideline. Exceptions to the rule are so numerous that the theories themselves are now under attack from both academics and industrialists. The plain fact is that some products do not grow, mature and die. Like Peter Pan, they never grow old. They are kept alive by the strength of their brand name and by the company's knack of rejuvenating them in the right way at the right time. The same is true of companies within a group. A 'cash cow' can be turned into a 'star' with the right leadership and understanding of the market. Almost any mature market is by definition ripe for picking – if you can evolve a sufficiently radical strategy or product that bypasses traditional ways of doing things. Who would have said the lawnmower market was anything but a stable cash cow until the first rotary electric mower entered the arena? It is also dangerous to assume that a mature business is a cash machine, as the theories suggest. Highly competitive, mature businesses frequently need a high level of investment.

What the individual manager can do   Whatever your business discipline, you can become a marketer too. Take the time and trouble to learn the basics of marketing (there is a wide variety of learning materials, from books to fully-fledged distance learning materials). Teach yourself not only the language of marketing, but the thinking of marketing.

If you can, try to include a spell in marketing or sales as part of your career development. Ask specifically to be seconded there for a period. Alternatively, seek to take on some market-oriented tasks, such as doing some initial market research into a new product idea you have proposed.

Take whatever opportunities offer themselves to get out and meet customers. Ask them what your department could do to help them. The answers you receive may be complete news to the marketing department, which may have been looking to the wrong people for its information, or asking the wrong questions. The manager of accounts receivable, for example, might find that the way the company provides credit facilities for certain types of customer can be changed to gain an advantage over or remove a disadvantage compared to the competition.

The combination of line management experience and marketing ability is worth a great deal in the promotion stakes in winning companies. If your company shows no signs of being a winner, the combination will still look good on your résumé when you move on.

BRAND STRENGTH

What the chief executive can do Creating strong brands is a little like creating a traditional English lawn: it takes years of care, attention and hard work. Once acquired, it requires constant maintenance to keep it in tip-top condition. Some brands have remained successful for fifty years or more.

Brands are, in one sense, a visible symbol of the company's standard of excellence, of the qualities people in the market associate with that product range. The detail of brand management is not for the chief executive to become embroiled in. There are, however, a number of things he can do both to build the brand name and to maintain it. Among these are:

● make the company name strong. Many companies try to build brand names solely around the product. But in buying the product, the customer is heavily influenced by a whole range of other assumptions about the company that made it. It is significant that those retailers who have been most successful with own-label goods are those who already have a strong company name to take the place of a conventional brand message on the packet, and support the product in a comparable way.

A sales-oriented company will often neglect to promote the company, concentrating solely on the individual products or product ranges. In doing so, it misses the chance of transferring customers' goodwill from one product to another. For example, ICI, in most respects now a highly successful company, has for years failed to capitalize effectively in its brand marketing on the high esteem in which the company as a whole is held.

To the customer, by and large, the company is its products; or in service industries, its people. You can make that link work for you, first by establishing a public image of your company that makes the customer feel comfortable, even secure, doing business with you. Then insist that both the company name and the product name are prominent on wrappings, promotional materials, advertisements and anything else that customers and distributors see. That doesn't mean you should necessarily impose a group name on units or divisions which already have a corporate identity of their own. The name Wiggins Teape, for example, is always likely to be stronger in the paper business than that of its parent company BAT. If you do not already do so, you should make sure that you receive regular comparative reports (at least every two years) that indicate

(1) the strength of the company name, both absolute and by comparison with major competitors
(2) the strength of the main product brand names, both absolute and by comparison with major competitors
(3) the strength of the link between them

This information will not only give you an insight into specific strengths and weaknesses in the marketplace, but it will allow you to take more effective strategic decisions on where to spend promotional resources.

● be consistent across all products. Part of the value of strong brands is that people have a clear concept of the values your company and your products stand for. An automobile dealer who has agencies on the same premises for both BMW and Lada is giving a conflicting message about the type of business and the type of customer he is seeking. Is he selling high-quality, high-priced goods or cheap and cheerful? The brand images people hold are almost always very simple, very subjective. The slightest hint of confusion over what the company is about devalues the brand. If your brand message is value for money, then everything you sell should fit that same description. If it is speed of service, the same applies. Before you launch any new product, examine it carefully to ensure it will not impair the coherence of the brand image. (As a matter of sheer practicality, any launch that does not fit the public concept of your company's 'patch' will usually be harder work and more expensive than one which clearly capitalizes on existing brand perceptions.)

● promote your brand name strongly at all times and especially when the market is depressed and the competition is cutting back. It's not just a matter of advertising spending – although that is important – but of maintenance and improvement of standards. The message 'Other manufacturers may be cutting corners to keep their costs down, but we refuse to compromise on the things that matter to the customer' can be remarkably powerful in developing brand loyalty. This approach is not cheap, but it demonstrates that your company regards itself as being in the business for the long term.

- support the brand by making sure the whole background to the product or service fits the brand image. If your company or brand image is one of technical competence and state-of-the-art technology, don't attempt to sell through technologically illiterate salespeople. Some of the personal computer companies found this out to their cost when trying to sell their products to businessmen through office equipment shops. Few, if any, of the sales assistants knew anything about computers and were completely unable to give the businessman advice on which machine would best meet his needs. (We recall one assistant in a major office equipment and stationery chain who, when asked if she stocked floppy disks, replied haughtily that all her furniture was very solid.) Those distributors that were specialist computer shops were primarily aimed at the home computer market and had little understanding of the businessman's problems. The 'cheap' sales image this created pushed the market into the hands of manufacturers whose company name was sufficiently associated with reliability, stability and technical expertise for the business customer to feel they were likely to be still in business in five years' time and would be able to help him resolve any difficulties he had in using his machine. Names such as Commodore and Osborne suffered by comparison. The IBM personal computer is not, by many accounts, either the best value for money or an outstanding machine in terms of what it can do. But the IBM name was enough to guarantee it the lion's share of a market characterized by consistent overselling of product virtues and by inferior product support and service arrangements. Significantly, the other big names to win through across Europe have been companies with similarly stable reputations, such as Hewlett-Packard and Olivetti. Only a handful of the *nouveaux arrivés* have retained significant market share.

The essence of brand strength is consistency.

What the individual manager can do Very little, where brands are concerned, unless you are the marketing manager. Then, of course, you do have a very strong influence on how brand strength is maintained. You should, for example, take great pains to ensure that the brand image and the company image are mutually supportive. It may sometimes mean pointing out weaknesses in other departments, which may not make you popular, but if you are not alert to anything that might affect the brand image, you are not doing your job. Remember, every reinforcement you create for the company/brand image is a reinforcement for your image inside the company as someone who understands and can operate effectively within the culture.

If you are a manager in another department you can also help reinforce the company/brand image by looking carefully at what happens within your department. Does everything that happens there reflect those qualities? If not, what are you going to to do about it?

CUSTOMER RELATIONS

What the chief executive can do   Relatively few manufacturing or service companies have customer relations managers, although most retailers do. Whether you have such a department or not, however, every complaint is your problem. You may not have to respond to it personally, but you should be certain that it is handled swiftly and well. After all, the badly handled complaint is a marketing disaster. Not only may that customer never darken your doors again, but he is likely to spread the word about how he has been treated. The well-handled complaint, on the other hand, can turn an angry and disappointed person into a walking advertisement for your company as surely as if you fitted him or her with sandwich boards.

That is why some excellence-minded companies have placed the handling of complaints directly in the hands of a senior manager, reporting directly to the chief executive. This manager's job is first to make sure that the chief executive knows about complaints. (In most companies they tend to be filtered out before they reach executive level, unless they are directed personally to the chief executive). The second part of his job is to make sure that all complaints are acted upon to the customers' satisfaction, as far as possible.

If you aim for your company to win through marketing, you cannot ignore the impact of complaints. You have to know how many people are complaining, what they are complaining about and what is being done to resolve and prevent complaints. To do this you must have some form of formal complaints-handling organization at a senior level. The lower down you delegate the responsibility, the less likely you are to know what is going on. Moreover, the aggrieved customer will react more positively to a letter signed by, say, the marketing director (or better still by you yourself) than one by someone of indeterminate or insignificant status in the company.

You also need a clear and consistent company-wide policy on what to do when a complaint is received: who handles it, how they deal with it, how swiftly they must respond, who should be copied in upon it. The policy should stress first that every complaint is an opportunity to cement relationships with the customer, and second that it is important to impress the customer from the start that his complaint is being treated with the seriousness that he considers it deserves. At that moment, as far as he is concerned, he is your only customer, and it pays to treat him as such.

Make sure all complaints are recorded and analysed. There are several reasons for doing this. One is that you will want to check out those that catch your eye and find out what was done about them. Another is so that you can trace patterns of complaints, and put pressure on the departments at fault to prevent them from recurring. A third is to check that the complaint really has been dealt with. (If the complaint is caused partly or wholly by a failure by a supplier, you should be able to check that *both* companies have contacted the customer. If the supplier's response is inadequate, your company will want to know, in order either to apply pressure or to deal with the matter instead.)

Educate both your employees and your customers in how to complain. The customers? Yes, because those you hear from are usually only those who were angry enough to sit down and write or telephone. How many dissatisfied customers are there out there, for whom complaining is too much bother, yet who are likely to switch to another brand next time they buy? Learn to use those who do complain as a valuable resource.

The idea of actually encouraging complaints may seem strange. But if you are aiming for excellence, you will want people to tell you when you miss the mark. So you should look to make it easier for customers to register complaints (and compliments, if they wish). You might print a special telephone number for handling problems on the packaging of your product or even, as Corning Glass once did, give customers a potted guide to how to complain in general.

You can test the effectiveness of your company's complaints-handling system in a number of ways. For example:

- get an outside agency to ring up with fictitious complaints or queries, and record what happens. Or do it yourself. If you have been left hanging on the line for 10 minutes or shunted between half a dozen departments, then you have a problem
- publish a selection of complaints, and how they were dealt with, in the employee newspaper, to reinforce the message throughout the organization
- even if you receive detailed reports on complaints, talk to complainants yourself sometimes – you may learn far more than appears in the report
- make sure the complaints-handling procedure includes provision for contacting the customer again to check whether he or she is satisfied with the action taken. You will never satisfy everyone entirely every time, but you need to be sure you are satisfying most complainants most of the time.

Although you will delegate most of these actions, you must insist that you are involved immediately whenever any really serious complaint occurs – not just because of its potential impact on the business, but because it pays to reinforce the impression within the organization of how seriously you take dealing properly with complaints. Be prepared to drop everything and look at the problem personally. It is not just the company's relationship with that customer, however important he may be, that is at stake; the reputation of the company is at stake, and that is very definitely your business.

We have spoken here almost entirely of complaints, but of course customer relations has its positive side, too. Your company can provide the customer with all sorts of supporting information and services that will increase the usefulness or enjoyment of the product. Very often this is designed as an afterthought – and it shows. The instruction manuals that come with most microcomputers, for example, are woefully inadequate. You can stress the quality difference between your products and the competition's by the quality of the support you supply. You can also insist that these materials and, services are designed into the product from its inception. For example a spare screw or button in the case of loss shows you care.

What the individual manager can do   The key to good handling of customer complaints is speed. The longer people have to stew over something, the angrier they become. Whatever the complaint, handle it *now*. Monitor how your staff deal with complaints, no matter whether the source is internal or external. If you are in a department such as production or assembly, where human error can produce particularly noticeable faults, get your subordinates to work with you to analyse all complaints as a means of improving quality control.

QUALITY CONTROL

What the chief executive can do   *Quality is free* is the title of a famous US book on quality control. Free it may be, up to a point, but easy it isn't. Maintaining consistently high quality is a never-ending but satisfying treadmill, requiring constant vigilance and continuous investment. On the other hand, there is now no excuse for the company that does not continue to improve quality, not just of its product, but in everything it does, from the invoices it sends out to the manner in which it delivers products. Automation, both on the shopfloor and in the office, is creating continuous opportunities for quality improvement, while most manufacturing firms now give at least lip service to the ability of properly motivated employees to come up with new quality control approaches. Any company that can't improve quality year by year in the 1980s is not standing still; it is regressing by comparison with the winners in its sector, who are constantly seeking new ways of raising their quality.

Among positive actions the chief executive can take are:

- have regular quality audits: How good is the quality of our products and services? How does it compare with the competition's?
- review the consistency of the quality image across the company. Does everything, from company stationery to the state of repair of the manufacturing plant, suggest a dedication to quality?
- encourage employees to participate in the quality development process. It is often forgotten that the origins of the much-discussed 'Japanese' techniques of quality circles and zero defects lie in the work of a US statistician, Dr W. Edwards Deming, who was invited to Japan in 1950 to help companies there overcome their reputation for producing cheap and shoddy goods. The international success of Japanese manufacturing firms since then has been due in considerable part to the concept of total quality

control. One of Deming's key principles is that 'Good quality does not necessarily mean high quality – it always means a predictable degree of uniformity and dependability at low cost with quality suited to the market.' In other words, a high level of quality control is just as applicable and necessary if you are making a Sinclair electric car as if you are making a Rolls-Royce. Another of Deming's principles – all of which are backed up by impeccable statistical evidence – is that increasing quality control actually reduces costs, contrary to the normal assumption that the last 3 per cent towards perfection always costs as much as or more than the first 97 per cent. A really thorough approach to quality, however, achieves savings in reworking and in scrap, while showing up where better design can reduce the numbers of components needed and the amount of materials that go into them.

Most British firms merely pay lip service to the possibility of achieving zero defects. Wilkinson Sword, on the other hand, rejects the notion of an acceptable level of imperfection and has used the philosophy of zero defects as a basis for reorganizing its production methods. The company urgently needed an economically priced razor which would challenge the Bic disposable, without damaging Wilkinson's reputation for quality goods. According to Derek Gatley, technical director at Wilkinson, 'The secret of quality control is never to accept a fault in products or components without recording it, analysing why it is wrong, feeding the information back and doing something about it.'

Wilkinson tries to reduce the likelihood of defects at every stage, before the product reaches the assembly line: 'We have a philosophy that you cannot *inspect* quality into a product – you must build it in,' explains Gatley. The role of quality controller has been taken on by assembly line workers. 'We have spread this philosophy through senior management down to the last assembly line worker until everyone is geared towards the thought "I am my own product quality controller",' says Gatley. Wilkinson claims the benefits are clearly quantifiable, in improved scrap and waste material ratios, sales figures, customer satisfaction and staff morale.

What the individual manager can do You too can maintain and improve quality by setting high standards both for yourself and for your department, and monitoring how well they are being achieved.

Don't let second-rate work slip through; raise Cain about it. Make sure people realize why something isn't up to quality and why that matters. If the results of quality control failures are not immediately obvious, arrange for a practical demonstration. If you were a worker on a car assembly line, wouldn't you take increased care installing braking systems if you saw the tangled wreckage of a vehicle whose brakes had not been assembled correctly? You might not be able to present such dramatic examples, but you could hire a video camera for a day and interview a few dissatisfied customers on how they felt about a product quality failure from your department.

If the company does not already capture the information, create your own record of faults and errors. Try to identify the patterns among them, then prepare for senior management an analysis of the causes and recommendations on how to eliminate them.

If a thing is worth doing well, it's usually worth doing *really* well.

HUNGER FOR MARKET INFORMATION

What the chief executive can do   The better you know your market, the better the strategies and tactics you can evolve to meet demand and block penetration by competitors. It seems obvious, yet so many firms are reluctant to spend real money on market research. Market research won't always prevent your new products from being flops; but it will improve your hit rate.

Do make sure the information gathered by market research is *used*. Too much market research data ends up in bottom drawers, because no one has the courage to face up to its findings. The research findings may, of course, be wrong – but if they are correct, the chances are high that the competition has come to similar conclusions and is even now using its research to prepare an attack strategy against you.

What the individual manager can do   You may not have funds to authorize formal market research. But you can make suggestions of ways to gather or interpret useful market data. Look at the information that comes into your department from outside. What is there that, with a little effort, could shed a slightly different light on your market?

MARKET-ORIENTED R&D

What the chief executive can do   As we shall see in the chapter on 'Winning through innovation', innovation is another area where the chief executive needs to take a strong role himself, if what comes out of the laboratories or development departments is to meet the real market needs. You have to make sure that the whole of the R&D department not only understands marketing goals, but embraces them enthusiastically. That is something of a tall order, but the fact that winning companies manage to do it is a sign that you can, too.

Among specific steps you can take are:

- make sure that at least some of the key people in the R&D department have marketing experience
- organize R&D around project teams, with a project manager who understands the market needs. Include on those teams representatives of production, finance, marketing and other relevant departments to prevent R&D from producing the wrong product. Early involvement of production, for example, can keep down machining or assembly costs, simply by influencing the component specifications. The more advanced the project is when production is consulted, the more difficult it is to make even minor changes in its composition.
- compare the efficiency of your R&D effort against that of the competition. It will probably be difficult to gather the data to make detailed comparisons, but you can normally assess whether they are, for example, getting more significant innovations per pound of their R&D spending, or whether they are getting their new products out of the lab faster than you are. Be careful to compare not just with the obvious competitors, but with major companies who have the ability to become competitors, if they wish. One of the most frequent failings of R&D departments is that they hang on to development projects too long. They lack the marketer's sense of urgency about getting the product to market first. You can raise the tempo of R&D by creating internal competition, by adjusting the incentive scheme to reward those who bring their projects in on or before time, and by giving people the autonomy to shut themselves away in small, action-oriented multi-disciplinary-groups where they can do things their own way. You can also emphasize the importance of speedy development by the speed

at which you give decisions to go ahead. If you have mulled over a properly researched project idea for six months before saying yes, the R&D staff can be expected to assume it is not that urgent, no matter what you say.

● monitor the process by which new products are produced. Are they getting the influence from marketing they need at the right time, or is marketing regularly making requests for changes at a late stage? While you can expect, if you are realistic, that as most new products will be failures, at least some of yours will go the same way, you should not shrug them off. Dissect each failure to see what can be learnt from it in terms of product development and launching. You may occasionally find that only a relatively minor adjustment to a product you were about to abandon can convert it into a winner.

● look at where the primary impulse for new products comes from. Does the idea originate in marketing, in R&D or jointly between them? While it is generally better to have a market looking for a product than a product looking for a market, there is great motivational value in having the majority of ideas emerge as a collaborative effort between marketing and R&D people. If both departments feel that they 'own' the idea, both will be committed to it and they will co-operate more fully.

● if the opportunity presents itself, allow R&D staff who come up with an idea to work their passage with it out of the lab doors and into the market. A few companies – among them a West German automobile manufacturer and an Italian heavy electrical company – have built pilot plants in the labs, allowing the R&D project team to hire production staff and run the line just as it would be in full production. By the time production is moved into the factory, most of the bugs are ironed out, and the R&D staff return to their benches with a much fuller appreciation of how they can make production management's job easier or more difficult.

What the individual R&D manager can do   Get out and get the feel of the product or service in the field. Really useful innovations almost all begin and end out there, rather than in the laboratory. The Racal technicians hauling heavy radio sets through the jungle have passed into the legend of that company so thoroughly that personal experience of the product in action in the real world is accepted as routine by the company's scientists and engineers. So it should be with you.

Step back from the routine of day-to-day development work every few weeks to look at each project from the point of view of the customer or end user. Go and experience the environment he or she will be operating it in. Remember the example of the hatchback car, which (so the story goes) was developed only when an automobile maker included a significant number of women on the design team. Previously, no one had thought to test cars out for convenience for the young mother with carrycot or pram.

You can ram this message home to your subordinates in a variety of ways. Gather examples of products that failed to look sufficiently closely at customers' and users' needs. For example, the computer terminal that burly steelmen couldn't operate properly because their fingers were too big for the keys. Or the two classically disastrous designs of telephone exchange. One reduced productivity because it was so quiet the operators couldn't chat without being overheard by the supervisor, which made them unable to relax. In the other, which had to be working twenty-four hours a day, the designers had forgotten to provide easy maintenance access, so technicians were obliged to crawl through the operators' legs. Make arrangements for short exchanges between some of your research staff and employees from major customers. Working in the customer's own premises, doing the job his employees do, can give invaluable insights.

Look for opportunities to develop new products with your customers, especially in the industrial sector. The pilot that works well in an existing customer's operations is more likely to succeed than one tested only in the laboratory. Assuming he is at least reasonably typical of the market, the earlier the customer is involved in the project and the more pleased he is with the product that emerges, the more marketable the product will be.

ACTION-ORIENTED MARKETING

What the chief executive can do The information you need about your market to make strategic decisions is becoming increasingly complex. You need to make use of all the modern tools available to present that information in a form where you can use your subjective experience of the market together with (what you hope is) more objective analytical data from market research and corporate planning.

Make use of the variety of computer-based decision support systems now becoming available to the executive suite. It is now possible to play modelling games on large screens, where you can compare your marketing strategy with that of each of your competitors.

Do also use the new technologies to improve your control of the marketing process. You can now directly access your customer's premises to determine what he needs, and your suppliers' to establish how swiftly they can deliver. By establishing control over the entire supply chain you can radically reduce the time it takes to react to change in the market. This applies to low-tech, mature markets as well as to the faster-moving high-tech industries.

What the individual manager can do The manager outside the marketing department can liaise closely with marketing to ensure that changes that might be necessary to meet new market conditions can be implemented rapidly. Even if you are not formally on a marketing committee, you can ask your peers in marketing for regular updates on significant market trends. Have yourself put on the routing list for relevant memos. Provide marketing, in return, with an estimate of the action you could take to meet changed needs and how long you would need to do so. For example, a call for a new pack size may involve the production department in machine adjustments, some minor expenditure on new equipment and advance warning to board suppliers. Having the information on costs and supply times to hand when the crisis breaks is one way of impressing top management with your ability to be on the ball.

6 Winning through getting back to basics (and staying there)

Knowing what business your company is in, why it is in that business and how it slots in to that market sector are all essential to the success-oriented company.

All companies accumulate habitual ways of doing and looking at things. Successful companies are no exception: the difference is that they have a clear idea *why* these basic attitudes and methods are important. They see certain values or principles as fundamental to their business, not because 'that's the way we've always done it', but because they recognize that these values provide a solid framework around which the business can be built. To use another common metaphor, these values are the compass that tells top management whether it is going in the right direction.

The vast majority of companies have given little or no thought to what the fundamental values of their businesses are or should be. The following questions will help you establish how far your company has progressed.

GENERAL QUESTIONS

1a Can you define closely, in one line and with confidence the business your company or operating unit is in?

b How long did you have to think about the previous question?

not at all
less than one minute
more than one minute

2 Does that definition encompass *all* the activities in your company's business portfolio?

3a Can you define closely, with confidence and in a few words the values that really matter in your company's business?

b How long did you have to think about the previous question?

> *not at all*
> *less than one minute*
> *more than one minute*

4 How well do you think middle and top management would agree with your definitions?

> *closely*
> *fairly closely*
> *not very*
> *don't know*

5 What procedures does your company have for comparing its activities against the fundamentals of the business?

> *regular reviews*
> *irregular reviews*
> *none*

6 Does your company provide all employees with a written statement of its basic values and principles?

7 If yes, does it deliberately reinforce that statement by frequent repetition and examples in other company media?

STICKING TO THE LAST

8 Does your company diversify by preference ...?

> *only within the areas it knows well*
> *into parallel areas where it already has some expertise*
> *into something completely different*

9   Is your company's predominant approach to diversification ...?

> *the dramatic leap into new pastures*
> *the continual re-establishment of commitment to existing product lines*
> *evolution based on perceived existing strengths*

10   Does the company's product portfolio contain ...?

> *virtually no ill-fitting products*
> *some ill-fitting products*
> *a lot of ill-fitting products*

11a   Are new product development and acquisitions carried out according to a clearly defined and well-understood set of rules?

b   When were those guidelines last overhauled?

> *within the past two years*
> *in living memory*
> *never*

c   Do those rules allow product managers to diversify wherever they see an opportunity?

12   Which of the following is true? Companies most often make bad diversifications ...

> *through inadequate preparation*
> *through lack of ideas to choose from*
> *through poor timing*

13   How many of your company's acquisitions become permanent parts of the group (i.e. are still there 10 years later)?

> *100 per cent*
> *80 per cent and more*
> *50 per cent and more*
> *less than 50 per cent*

14   Can you honestly say that most of your company's acquisitions ...?

> *are successes*

*do not normally improve greatly as a result of their new ownership
are failures*

15   Which of the following is true? Acquisitions are most likely to
succeed if . . .

*the two companies share the same technological base
the two companies share different but similar technological bases
the two companies are both in the same markets
the two companies are in different markets*

ATTENTION TO DETAIL

16   How does your company react to minor defects in its products?

*raise Cain until they are fixed and make sure it never happens
again
raise Cain until they are fixed, then forget about it till the next
time
accept it as inevitable unless a major customer complains loudly
enough
try to bury the matter as quickly as possible*

17   How comprehensive are your company's procedures for analysing mistakes and making sure they do not recur?

*very comprehensive
patchy
non-existent*

18   Do you have the information in your job to detect the difference
between whether everything you have responsibility for has been
done right, and whether it has merely been done almost right?

19   Does the company folklore contain well-circulated stories of the
virtues of attention to detail?

EYE ON THE BALL

20 How often does your company examine its 'sacred cows' – its untouchable policies or departments – to see whether they still belong in its core objectives?

> *frequently*
> *occasionally*
> *never*

21 You see that a senior manager's bright idea isn't working. Would the best option in your company culture be to ...?

> *tell him yourself*
> *write a signed memo to his superior*
> *write an anonymous memo to his superior*
> *keep your head down and make sure you are not involved when the balloon goes up*

22 How long does it normally take between the realization that what seemed like a good idea isn't working and actually doing something about it?

> *weeks at most*
> *months*
> *years*
> *forever*

23 How many major mistakes is your company still living with?

> *a lot*
> *a few*
> *none*

24 Does your company habitually ...?

> *test ideas thoroughly in the marketplace, with the acceptance that it will pull back rapidly if they fail*
> *assume ideas will work and examine them thoroughly only when they are under way*

25 Does your company's culture reward people more ...?

> *for pulling out of disappointing projects at the first sign of trouble*
> *for pulling out as soon as it is obvious the project is a failure*
> *for carrying on to prove the point*

26 When did your company last ask its market what *it* thinks you do well?

> *within the last two years – we do it regularly*
> *more than two years ago*
> *never*

POINTS TO WATCH:

Question 9: the third alternative is the correct one. Great leaps forward carry a great likelihood of falling flat on your face. Over-emphasis on existing products can be fatal. Strategically, what counts is less the products you make than the business you are in.

Question 11c: while the demands of autonomy and innovation argue for freedom to explore new areas, the search needs to be controlled to prevent effort being wasted on ideas that do not fit the fundamentals of the business

Question 12: although there is in theory no shortage of good ideas, in practice very few *good* ideas reach top management, and most of those that do are both inadequately prepared and unlikely to fit well into the fundamentals of the business

Question 15: none of the answers is correct. All these factors have to be considered on a case-by-case basis. The key element in most successful acquisitions is whether the acquisition strategy will achieve real added value, for example through clearly identified cost savings.

GENERAL POINTS

What the chief executive can do Like control and autonomy, zero basing and innovation are at least superficially opposites. You have to do a balancing act between holding fiercely to principles that matter, while encouraging everyone in the organization to question and experiment with those that do not matter. The trick, of course, is understanding exactly what the core values of your company are.

To you and every key manager in your organization, those core values have to be instinctive – a knee-jerk reaction. That's why it is important to make sure everyone knows what the basic principles of the business are, and to reinforce them at every opportunity. Look at the employee newspaper, if you have one. Do the stories reflect the corporate values you consider important, in a way that the readers will find credible? Does top management make a habit of putting its plans and actions in the context of those basic principles, when it talks to groups of employees?

A number of the successful firms described in *The Winning Streak* have expressed their basic values, their 'statement of mission' as a formal, regularly repeated item in their annual report, or issued them to employees as a separate booklet either when they join the firm or whenever a minor adjustment is made to the core values. This removes the excuse 'How am I supposed to know what you want of me?' and gives a ready reference everyone can turn to.

These company 'Bibles' need not be tablets of stone. They can and do change in detail, although rarely in any of the basics. Moreover, they do not have to be handed down from on high, enshrined in mystery. STC went out of its way to consult its employees about the nature and contents of its proposed statement of mission. You may not need to conduct such a wide-ranging participative exercise, but it does make sense to consult with at least a representative sample of employees regarding the kind of values they would be able to accept and – most importantly – to respect. One of the surprises you are likely to encounter is the strength of feeling that people have about setting high values to live up to. Areas in which the company is manifestly weak may be of more concern to employees at the lowest level than to middle or even senior management. For example, the person whose job perforce involves providing an inferior level of customer service has to live with it day in, day out. It affects his whole attitude to the organization ('If they can't look after the customer, they're not going to look after me'), and that affects his general motivation. The core values that emerge will almost certainly reflect where people think the company ought to be rather than where it is.

Of course, your company probably has a few slogans buried around its buildings, espousing virtues that are close if not identical to the core values you want to inculcate. The chances are high, however, that they have been devalued through disuse or misuse. You may have to go through an extensive programme of re-education and re-affirmation of values to overcome employees' natural suspicion that they are just being served with the same hypocritical clap-trap yet again. It's no good having core values without living up to them.

As a simple checklist on how to present the company's core values, the following points may be helpful:

- keep it as simple and practical as possible. Long-winded philosophical ramblings are no match for straightforward statements back up by example.
- make sure these are values people in the organization can accept. If they are not with you, they are against you.
- make full use of the existing culture of the organization and the principles the employees themselves feel to be important

Once you have such a set of guidelines, you can use them as a yardstick against which to measure virtually everything that happens in your company.

What the individual manager can do How well do you understand the basic principles by which your company operates? You can make sure by asking visiting top management to expand on the theme, if possible in the presence of key subordinates. If you do understand the principles, how well are they actually being applied in your department?

Because the company statement of mission, assuming it has one, will inevitably be very broadly based to cover all departments and activities across the organization, you have considerable room for manoeuvre in creating a departmental set of values. These will apply the principles of the corporate values to the work of your department, expanding them where necessary, giving examples wherever possible.

You will find them of value both in assessing your own work and in directing and advising subordinates on theirs.

STICKING TO THE LAST

What the chief executive can do   One of the problems with 'wall-hopping', in which a company jumps from one field to another where the grass looks greener, is that the greener the grass, the more likely it is to be a bog. The fact is that relatively few diversifications work well, and even fewer acquisitions. According to *Fortune* magazine, eight out of ten acquisitions turn out to be blunders.

It's surprising how few companies have concise and well-thought-through diversification and acquisition policies. Some of those that do concentrate on the characteristics of the new activity, sparing relatively little thought for those of the existing organization. Yet there must be a close match between the two for the venture to have a realistic chance of success.

There are actually two starting points for any effective diversification/acquisition policy. One is 'What are we good at?' The other is 'Where do we want to be in five or ten years' time?' – top management's vision of the future. Any diversification or acquisition that does not draw its principal justification from both of these criteria probably isn't worth pursuing. There may well be a profitable business there. But is it right for your company? The ability to walk away from a venture that isn't right is just as important as being able to seize the opportunities that really do fit. As Dr Rolf Berth of the International Management Institute stresses, many poor decisions to diversify or acquire are made simply because the range of viable alternatives presented to top management is so meagre. You can overcome the tug-of-war between sticking to what you know and the need to innovate, by increasing the choice of new ventures that reaches you.

One simple, but rarely undertaken, means of doing so is to publish the diversification and acquisition rules internally, inviting at least every manager to make proposals, pass on intelligence and so on. You may also obtain remarkable co-operation from your trade unions if you assure them that the objective is to provide additional jobs through expansion. By explaining to people what you are looking for and why, you will generate a substantial volume of ideas with a much higher 'fit' rate. Remember, the vast majority of employees will have spouses, aunts, uncles and second cousins, some of whom will be working for other companies you might acquire or which might have interesting ideas for joint ventures. By using the employees as another antenna into the outside world you can greatly increase your awareness of the opportunities there.

Having a greater choice of direction, within clear guidelines, means that you can judge more clearly what you want to acquire, and, equally importantly, avoid being pressurized into paying too much for it. The standard justification put forward for virtually every major acquisition these days seems to be in terms of 'synergy' – 'There will be a great deal of synergy between the two product ranges' or 'The management philosophies of the two companies are highly synergistic.' What all this usually boils down to is that the two companies think they can get along together. The real test, says PA Strategy Partners' Jim Lawrence, is whether combining organizations will save costs.

The better you (and everyone else in the organization) understand the business you are in, the easier you will find it to stick to your particular last. In particular it will be easier to establish swiftly whether a diversification or acquisition really is building on existing strengths. The same applies, of course, to demergers. The less easily something sits within the basic business pattern of the company, the more of the top executives' time it is likely to take up – which makes it a weakness. If you have enough alternative high-return investment choice in the areas you know, the ill-fitting business has to be exceptionally profitable to avoid becoming an opportunity cost.

What the individual manager can do   'I'm always coming up with viable new product ideas, but they are never implemented.' Could that be you? The explanation might be that the company isn't interested in innovating or diversifying. Equally, it may be that your ideas do not build sufficiently on existing strengths and know-how, i.e. they do not meet the criterion of sticking to the last. The closer you understand the basic guiding principles of the business, the more likely you are to come up with ideas that will be accepted. If in doubt, ask top management to outline the characteristics they are looking for in new products or new ventures. If they can't give a clear explanation, then you know the fault lies at least partially with the company. Then you should consider the option of taking your ideas (and yourself) elsewhere.

It can be a valuable exercise from time to time for you to go back to basics on everything you do in your department. Why do we do this in this way? Why do we do it at all? Some accountants have been proselytizing zero-base budgeting for years, with a certain amount of success. But zero basing everything is a far less common concept. We talked in the chapter on controls about putting 'sell by' dates on all control systems, to ensure that a specific decision had to be taken to continue them. Those that have become obsolete are automatically weeded out in this process. That same principle can be applied across the whole range of activities under your control. Asking 'Why do we do this?' can throw up a remarkable number of activities whose purpose has been lost.

ATTENTION TO DETAIL

What the chief executive can do   All the things that matter in your company need personal, frequent attention from you. While you cannot afford to become embroiled in the nitty-gritty of day-to-day operations, you must and should demonstrate that it's the little things that make the difference between doing a job adequately and doing it well. You can create company folklore by the actions you take. Make a point of picking up minor things which aren't quite right. And follow them up to make sure that they are remedied.

Of course, your objective is not to find fault for its own sake, so the errors you remark upon must be genuine and you must genuinely regard them as important. After all, you are creating or reinforcing culture each time you jump on something in this way. You can train yourself to look for the right issue and to handle it in a manner that explains to people *why* it is important. Make them, for example, put themselves in the customer's shoes. For example, 'How would you feel if you received that letter?' 'Suppose it were you who injured yourself on that pile of scrap?' The fact that you take the personal trouble to deal with the matter indicates to employees that they really must take it seriously themselves.

You can capitalize on these situations most effectively on the spot, when you are visiting plants and offices. But you can also pick up a great deal from your own management information systems – if they collect the right data and you ask the right questions.

One of the principal reasons why many companies find it hard to monitor detail is that the vast majority of mistakes are hidden. The culture of these companies holds out only punishment for those who admit to having made mistakes. Concealment becomes an essential part of survival. As a result, not only do mistakes become compounded while those responsible hope they will either not be noticed or will rectify themselves, but the company loses many valuable opportunities for people to learn from each other's mistakes.

You can create an environment where the frank and ready admission of mistakes is rewarded rather than punished, where the worst crime is to conceal bad news. Get into the habit of analysing mistakes with senior managers, not to apportion blame, but to establish what can be learnt to prevent a recurrence. Impress upon them the need to do the same with their subordinates and on down the line. Encourage people not only to admit that something has gone wrong, but to come forward with their own proposals to remedy it.

What the individual manager can do Like the chief executive, you can establish an example for your subordinates to follow. If they know you will never check on something, their motivation to make sure it is exactly right is unlikely to be high. On the other hand, if you make a habit of spot-checking, you will maintain their awareness of the need to do it right all the time.

The control systems imposed on your department from outside will probably not have been designed with the primary objective of keeping you informed of what is going on (though they should have been), but to provide the information senior management wants. If that is so, there will be numerous small gaps, where the detail of the department's work is not being monitored. You should look to establish where those gaps are and how they can be plugged. You can also involve the employees themselves in the process of monitoring detail. Get them to criticize things that don't seem quite right, to inform you of anything they consider not up to standard. And ask them to make suggestions for how they could be put right or prevented from happening again.

Remember that the purpose of attention to detail is not to seek perfection for its own sake. That would not only be rather pointless; it would also be extremely boring. No, the purpose of attention to detail is to make sure that everything the company does complements or enhances its basic business principles, rather than undermines them.

EYE ON THE BALL

What the chief executive can do Few of us enjoy being criticized; even fewer are capable of being dispassionate self-critics. If we look at the case histories of many unsuccessful companies, however, we see that one of the primary causes of their decline or demise is top management's inability to take a really critical look at their company and where it is going.

If you are to avoid making this mistake, you must:

- take regular opportunities to remove yourself from your normal work routines and try to look in at the company as if you were an impartial observer. By all means use outside consultants to hold the mirror up to your company, but that on its own is rarely enough for you to really *feel* how your company appears to outsiders.
- be open to – indeed invite – constructive criticism of your strategies and policies. The youngest managers in the company are likely to be the most hypercritical. Attend their training sessions, explain how you see the company and ask them to take that vision apart with you. Challenge their assumptions and get them to challenge yours. Those chief executives who have the courage to expose themselves to this kind of battering rarely end up changing their minds about any fundamental aspects of the business – not least because only those who have really thought through and criticized these things themselves will have the confidence to do it. But the process does throw up a lot of minor matters in which improvements may be valuable. Even more important, it increases the standing of the chief executive among the junior management ranks.
- make it clear that you expect other managers to expose their plans, strategies and values to open criticism in the same way. Unless people know they can speak their mind without fear of subsequent victimization, they will hold their tongues rather than risk pricking a more senior manager's bubble. You have to

convince everyone not only that it is safe to speak up, but that it is their duty to do so. You may have to intervene personally to protect an employee whose manager takes exception to a dissenting voice in his department: certainly, there should be no hesitation on your part in doing so. Better to let the professional carper sound off than to prevent the employee with a genuine objection or alternative view from expressing his opinion.

- make every new idea undergo a baptism of fire, not to kill it but to ensure that it has been thoroughly thought through against established principles before it is presented to top management. Managers in several of the companies described in *The Winning Streak* never present half-thought-out plans more than once. The trauma of having all one's assumptions tested mercilessly makes a lasting impression. So does the elation when a plan passes all the tests.

- never throw good effort after bad. The moment an apparently good idea turns out to have been a bad one, chop it. The temptation to hang on until a disappointing venture 'turns the corner' is difficult to resist, especially if it was your idea and you have a great deal of emotional capital tied up in it. That's why it's important for you both to criticize and to accept criticism. If you can't admit 'I screwed up on this one', how can you expect anyone else in the organization to do so? When you conduct the project post-mortem, insist on answers to three questions: What made us think this was a good idea in the first place? Why did it take so long for us to realize our mistake? Could we have spiked it any faster?

- evaluate all new ventures against basic principles at regular intervals, and certainly immediately before the final decision to launch. While you do not want your company to gain a reputation for never having the courage to jump the last hurdle to market, neither can you afford to have a string of expensive failures. If you have been evaluating the project against basic principles from the start, however, it will normally require a major external change in the market for you to abort at that late stage. It seems like plain common sense to test new products or services in the marketplace before launching for real. The experience gained in one small area of the country can and frequently does make the difference between success and failure nationally. Yet many products are still launched directly on to the national or international market without a pilot phase, the excuse being that there is either no time or no money for a significant test. That is an excuse you cannot afford to tolerate. In the end, the person who decides whether the resources are available is you.

● identify the 'sacred cows' in your organization – the departments or practices that no one dares to question. How many of them are really valid now, when set against the core values of the company and the overall top management vision?

● identify your company's major mistakes in the past ten years, and make sure you are not still living with them. If a venture didn't meet the basic business principles then, and still doesn't after several years, it almost certainly never will, and it doesn't belong in your portfolio. Just as the evil that men do lives after them, so in most companies do the ghosts of the really big blunders. Sometimes the lessons from them are highly relevant today. More often than not, however, the wrong moral has been drawn. For example, a disastrous product launch into a particular new market will typically be interpreted by the management hierarchy as a sign that the environment there is hostile to their company. That may be totally untrue, a self-serving excuse for a failure in zero basing. Just because one product failed, you should not let that preclude you from looking at that market again, under changed conditions, with a different product. You, as chief executive, can oblige people to confront these historical calamities honestly and can insist that the correct lesson is drawn.

What the individual manager can do Whether or not your company is one that welcomes constructive criticism, the place to start is with yourself. Just how good are you at taking and acting upon such criticism? Ask your colleagues and your immediate superior. Don't be surprised if they say you are much less responsive to criticism than you thought you were. Wade through the piles of annual appraisal forms gathered by the personnel offices of any large company, and you will find that 'He finds it difficult to take criticism' is one of the commonest of negative comments.

Go out of your way to invite peers, colleagues and subordinates to dissect and criticize your ideas and proposals and show you are listening to what they have to say. By all means defend your ideas strongly – that's essential if you wish to demonstrate how committed to them you are – but be prepared to admit defeat when you are clearly wrong. Like the chief executive, you have got to be able to say 'I screwed up'. You should also be able to say 'And this is what I'm going to do about it.'

7 Winning through innovation

'For most people, most corporations and to most management, innovation is an extremely uncomfortable and extremely difficult process. The reason is that, fundamentally, innovation is by definition
both disruptive and revolutionary.' (John Dembitz, director of Charter-
house Japhet.)

Of all the desirable characteristics of management, innovation is
probably the hardest to achieve. People and organizations alike are
resistant to change. But like starting a car by pushing it, after a while
(with luck) the engine starts and the car moves off. You have to leap
aboard and start controlling it, or it will race away and cause havoc.
Companies with the winning streak appear to have set the wheels
turning and have jumped into the driving seat before they move too
fast.

Before you can make innovation work for your company you have
to establish how hard it will be to get the vehicle moving. The following questions will help you measure the inertia of your company.

GENERAL QUESTIONS

1   Does success belong to the company that innovates . . .?

> *first in its business sector*
> *second in its business sector*
> *last in its business sector*
> *sometimes first, sometimes second in its business sector*

2   What proportion of your company's sales turnover goes into
R&D?

a   manufacturing industry:

> *over 5 per cent*
> *3 to 5 per cent*

1 to 3 per cent
less than 1 per cent

b   service industry:

over 3 per cent
1 to 3 per cent
under 1 per cent
none at all

3   Do you have a policy for innovation?

4   Does your company have long-term innovation objectives (i.e. does it have a clear idea of the products it expects to sell after those you are researching now become obsolete)?

5   Does your company see innovation as ...?

just a matter for R&D
affecting every aspect of the organization

6   How strongly does innovation figure in the corporate strategy for your company?

very much
a little
the word isn't mentioned

7   Do your company's top managers

a   have a reputation for being innovators...?

b   identify where they want to innovate...?

very clearly
vaguely
not at all

8   List the five key developments in your industry over the past ten years. Did your company ...?

embrace them all immediately
dismiss some initially as of minor significance
dismiss most initially as of minor significance

9   Are there departments in your company which appear never to innovate?

FEW BARRIERS TO CHANGE

10   Does your company . . .?

reward managers for valuable new ideas
assume that innovation is part of the job description and does not
merit additional reward

11   Your company has had an expensive failure in a particular
market or technology sector. Does it . . .?

evaluate why things went wrong and invite people to suggest ways
of doing it better next time
cut its losses and refuse to countenance any forays into that sector
again

12   What proportion of managers in your company have been given
training in creativity techniques?

100 per cent
more than 30 per cent
less than 30 per cent

13   When faced with a revolutionary but apparently sensible new
idea does your company typically . . .?

look to see if it can be tested without great expense
keep referring it back for 'further evaluation'
decide it is 'too radical'

14   What happens to persistent mavericks in your company?

they are promoted quickly
they are promoted till someone chops their heads off for being
disruptive
we encourage them to move to a more suitable employer

15   Do shopfloor employees have guarantees that labour-saving
ideas they generate will not mean that they lose their jobs?

16   Has your company enthusiastically embraced quality circles or
other methods of encouraging ideas from below?

17a Is there a clear, formal structure for reviewing and testing new ideas?

b Does everyone know what that structure is?

18a When a dynamic young manager with lots of ideas quits, does your company attempt to establish why he felt he had to go elsewhere to further his career?

b Does the evidence you have suggest that these people mainly leave . . .?

> *because their ideas have been evaluated, but do not fit the corporate portfolio*
> *because no one will act on one of their ideas, although it has been evaluated positively*
> *because no one will listen to their ideas at all*

19a How fast do new ideas move through the corporate hierarchy from junior management to board level?

> *within days*
> *within weeks*
> *within months*
> *most never get there*

b And how fast does the initial response come down?

> *within days*
> *within weeks*
> *within months*
> *what response?*

20 You are told tomorrow that there will be major changes in your part of the company and that the content (though not the status or salary level) of your job will be affected. Is your reaction most likely to be . . .?

> *excitement at the prospect of tackling something new*
> *excitement tinged with worry*
> *sheer panic*

NATURAL CURIOSITY ABOUT HOW THINGS ARE DONE ELSEWHERE

21   How close a watch does your company keep on the development activities of the competition?

very close: we know their R&D programmes in great detail
quite close: we monitor them regularly
not closely at all: we just read the trade papers
not at all: we don't believe they are doing anything of interest

22   How long does it take for your company to follow up an interesting new idea elsewhere, to see if the idea could be applied to its own operations?

a couple of days or less
a month or less
up to a year
only when everyone else is doing it

INTERNATIONAL PERSPECTIVE

23   Does your company regard international conferences and symposia mainly as . . .?

a vital opportunity to keep up to date with what other people are doing
a reward for good performance
a waste of time

24   Has your company established international links for the specific purpose of keeping up to date with threats and opportunities from overseas?

25a   How many board directors have international experience (i.e. working at a senior level overseas)?

all
more than half
less than half
none

b How much time on average do board members spend overseas?

40 per cent or more
20 per cent or more
5 to 20 per cent
less than 5 per cent

26 If you are a technology-based firm, do you have an internal engineer or scientist able to scan the Japanese technical literature in Japanese?

27 Which is true? The easiest way to find out about long-term threats to your business from Japan is to ...

conduct extensive monitoring in Japan
read and analyse all trade reports and publications
ask the Japanese themselves
ask the US and UK chambers of commerce in Tokyo

DIRECTED R&D

28 Does top management set clear commercial objectives for R&D?

29 What proportion of junior R&D staff could tell you the market and production cost objectives for the products they are working on?

100 per cent
75 per cent plus
50 per cent plus
25 per cent plus
less than 25 per cent

30 Are project teams concerned with new product development and business development ...?

located on a single business site, with easy access to all the key business functions
isolated with frequent communications with other functions
isolated with infrequent communications with other functions

THE ROLE OF THE CHIEF EXECUTIVE

31a   How often does top management visit the laboratories/research facilities?

> *daily*
> *weekly*
> *monthly*
> *once in a blue moon*
> *never*

b   On these occasions does it . . .?

> *talk to small groups or individuals at any level*
> *talk to department heads*
> *talk to the R&D manager only*

32   Is the executive responsible for R&D . . .?

> *on the board of directors*
> *one layer below the board*
> *two or more layers below the board*

POINTS TO WATCH:

Question 1: first to market doesn't always win; indeed, it can be an expensive and risky approach. Companies with the winning streak tend to innovate first where it really matters, second where it is less important.

Question 23: if you chose the second answer, you've probably got a lot of bored and frustrated executives. If you want them to relax, send them on a paid holiday. Give them a single major problem to think about and ask them for a one-page report on it a week after they return. Send them to international conferences as well, of course, but to work and listen.

Question 25b: if you answered 40 per cent or more, who's minding the shop? It's very rare that any but the international director or export director needs to be overseas that much. A good average for most businesses is 15 to 25 per cent. There are people who can use air travel as thinking time, but they are few and far between.

Question 27: strangely enough, you simply have to ask the Japanese themselves. The local representative office of the Ministry of International Trade and Industry will supply you with a copy (in English) of Japan's plans for your industry.

Question 30: actually, the correct answer is the third. One of the lessons of *In Search of Excellence* is that effective project teams, having once been given clear guidelines and containing the inter-disciplinary skills, work best if they are cut off and left to it. Peters and Waterman refer to these isolated teams as 'skunkworks'.

GENERAL POINTS

Innovation rarely, if ever, just happens. It requires imagination, co-ordination and a sense of purpose. Sad to say, a great many boardrooms lack some or all of those qualities. So it's not that surprising that some companies find it hard to innovate.

Before we look at how you – as chief executive or as an ordinary manager – can create an environment where innovation will flourish, we should first demolish several common and highly pervasive myths. The first is that *innovation is the province of specific departments, notably research and development*. Experience across a wide range of companies shows that, in reality, even technological innovations depend for their success upon innovation in other functions such as marketing and production. Innovation is a process that properly involves everyone in the company, from shopfloor to boardroom.

The second myth is that *the essence of innovation is having ideas*. Not true. It is quite probable that everybody in your firm has at least one valid idea the company could conceivably make use of. The problems lie in drawing them out of people in a manner in which they can be properly evaluated, in making sure the inevitable filtering mechanism within the organization does not reject the really viable ones, and in bringing them to fruition. More precisely, innovation is about putting the right idea into practice at the right time and selling it in the right way. The idea is merely the starting point, and there are a great many hurdles to jump before it becomes a successful innovation. As we discussed briefly earlier, the paradox is that, in spite of the abundance of ideas inside and outside the company, top management in most companies actually receives far too few viable ideas for innovation.

Another common myth is that *continuous innovation is the province primarily of the high-tech industries*. In reality, the mature industries often show the greatest opportunity for innovation. Wherever established ways of doing things have become heavily ingrained, the regular march of progress is almost certain to throw up better ways. Radical new approaches to steelmaking, for example, now hold out the prospect of enabling that beleaguered industry in the US and Europe to compete on more equal terms with developing countries where labour and energy costs are low. Similarly, a growing number of companies in distribution have used advances in information technology to seize a strong hold on specific markets. In the United States, for example, the Hospital Corporation of America has locked out most of its competitors in the area of pharmaceutical supply by providing hospitals with a computerized ordering service. The service not only reorders drugs automatically, so the hospital pharmacy is never out of stock, but saves on the hospital's staffing costs. Most of these hospitals are now dependent on HCA for almost all their supplies.

The fourth common myth is that *most companies need to innovate only in order to get out of trouble*. The company that waits that long is in deeper trouble than it imagines. As the hospital example above demonstrates, innovation is now a strategic issue and needs to be treated as such. The alternative choices facing tomorrow's company are to seek competitive edge through effective use of innovation, or to risk being outflanked by a faster-moving, more innovative competitor. Could your company afford to be shut out of a large part of its market?

The fifth and last myth is that *innovation is cheap*. It is almost always more expensive than initially estimated. Moreover, most innovations take a while to pay off, and during that time they are likely to be a drain on profits or cashflow or both. It is therefore of little value to pay lip service to innovation without providing the resources to fund it not just in the ideas and investigation stages, but beyond into implementation and the long haul to market viability. That seems obvious, you may say. Yet, along with inadequate market research, insufficient funding is the most common reason for the failure of product innovations.

What the chief executive can do   If innovation is to become part of the fabric of a company's culture, it has to be taken seriously by everyone. All employees have to be aware that top management is committed to innovation as a means of progress and competitive advantage.

You will therefore need to establish a clear policy and objectives for innovation. It's no use just telling people to innovate blindly. To be really useful, innovation has to operate within defined objectives. Top management needs to spell out to employees where the company is now; where it wants to be in terms of size, type of product and kind of organization; and the kind of innovations it requires to take it there.

The employees (and also the suppliers, if you have the confidence to involve them in this way) also need to know that their contribution is genuinely wanted. The limitation on corporate funds obviously limits the number of ideas the company can pursue. But involvement in innovation is a many-staged affair. At every stage of implementation, new, usually minor but sometimes quite significant innovations need to be made. Without all these smaller innovations by ordinary people, the big ideas either will not work or will not work half as well.

You need to keep plugging away at the innovation theme. Keep reminding people that innovation is important, and they will keep responding to the challenge. But if you slacken the message off, they will assume you have lost interest. So echo it wherever possible in company literature.

Most people like to work for an innovative company – particularly the bright youngsters you most want to attract. When shoe manufacturer C. & J. Clark let the television cameras in on the progress of a new product development, it was not in the least dismayed when the development project failed. On the contrary, it was delighted at the flood of high-calibre job applications it received from television viewers who were impressed that a company in such an apparently low-technology industry could give a thirty-two-year-old man the chance to lead a major project. The programme certainly also had a good effect in encouraging people inside the firm to push for further innovations.

The innovation policy sets out the main ground rules for managing innovation. Among other things, it should spell out where the company wants to be in the innovation stakes. Does it want to be the leader, with all the benefits that entails in terms of high market profile? Or does it want to be a less exposed follower?

The problem with being an innovation leader is that it is expensive. Not only do you have all the development costs, but you also have to overcome the acceptance barriers within the market – again, often a costly exercise. 'Innovating second' allows you to watch your competitors remove the bugs and make the market aware of the product or service, before you launch into the same market having learnt from his mistakes. 'Innovating last' is a recipe for failure, because the key players in the market will normally by then have an unassailable position. Few companies have the financial and sales muscle of an IBM to allow them to take over a substantial portion of a mature market simply on the strength of the brand name.

While it pays to innovate first sometimes, if only to maintain the organization's sense of pride in its ability to develop successful new ideas, the drain on resources may be enormous. One option we recommend is that the innovation policy spells out the circumstances in which it wishes to innovate first and those in which it wishes to innovate second. The aim is to seek a balance between the two that allows your company to retain its reputation as an innovation leader without bankrupting itself through rushing headlong into uncertainty on too many fronts.

Andrew Robertson, a researcher at the Polytechnic of Central London, describes these two options as offensive and defensive innovation, pointing out that defensive innovators spend on average only half as much on fundamental research and 60 per cent on applied research as offensive innovators. He also points out that

> ... many managers seem to believe that 'first to market wins'. In most cases this is a myth. The exceptions are to be found in a handful of large-scale process industries like industrial chemicals, where an original process which cuts costs and improves quality can compel competitors to consign their older process plants to the mothballs. Two examples: the plate-glass industry revolutionized by Pilkington's float-glass process, and the chemical industry, where Standard Oil of Ohio's acrylonitrile process caused similar upheavals.

The choice of whether to innovate first, or offensively, is therefore primarily strategic, and relates both to the threats and opportunities the company foresees and to the resources it has to meet them. You can't normally advance in all directions. First top management has to take those strategic decisions, then it has to communicate them in policy terms as guidelines for people lower down the organization to search out specific opportunities.

One other thing the policy document should make clear is that, where the company innovates second, or defensively, it will only in the rarest circumstances be willing merely to imitate. However good someone else's idea may be, it is always capable of improvement. Ensuring that it is improved should be a matter of pride – and that, in this context, is far from an irrelevant consideration, for pride is a major component in the motivation of the typical person to generate and participate in innovation.

Other essentials are:

- the commitment of adequate resources to make innovation work. As we have already seen, innovation is expensive and can all too easily be throttled by lack of funding. Managers at all levels have to perform a balancing act between funding too few innovations, with the result that people feel their chances of having an idea accepted are too small to be worth the candle, and funding too many, with the risk that the available cash will be spread too thinly. Because innovation is needed across the company, rather than just in R&D, every manager should have a discretionary budget, which he can invest in pursuing new ideas. Most of this cash may be lost, when the ideas are abandoned or put on ice. But it will rarely be wasted, because, in the experience of many companies that follow this procedure, the revenue from the most viable and easily implemented ideas easily pays back the costs of the exercise as a whole. Much of this discretionary budget may be used to investigate ways of cutting costs, rather than of developing new products. If the savings can be left with the manager who makes them, as an addition to his discretionary budget, it will be another powerful motivator to keep the innovation cycle going. No company's budget should be considered acceptable if it does not contain a healthy allocation for 'revenue investment'.

- explaining the skills base of the company. It is surprising how ignorant many people in large companies are of the capabilities the organization has to produce new products or services. Making people aware of the centres of excellence that the company has, and how they can be tapped for the purposes of innovation, can give rise to all sorts of unlikely but profitable combinations of expertise. Among techniques already in use in a number of companies to ensure that their technology base is understood across the organization are technical bulletins aimed at detailing

resources available and whom to contact, regular conferences of
managers from different plants to discuss specific innovations
they have made, and internal technical 'open days'.

What the individual manager can do First, look at your department's reputation within the company. Is it seen by other managers
as a change leader ('Those guys will try anything new'), or a persistent follower ('They'll never do anything until someone else has
proved it's safe')? Ask other managers for their opinions. If nothing
else, it will make them see you in a different light. Even if your
department's reputation for innovation is high, there is probably a
good deal you can do to raise it further. For a start, you can make
sure your subordinates come up with a flow of ideas, by telling them
what you are looking for, and by listening and responding to the
suggestions they make.

When you have an idea that needs approval from higher up, your
most likely stumbling block is getting busy senior managers to give
it the attention you believe it deserves. You can teach yourself how
to present your ideas so that they will have a better than even chance
of being considered in detail. First, the idea should be encapsulated
into a very brief summary of less than one page in one-and-a-half-
spaced typing. The summary should explain in simple terms (top
management doesn't have the time to refer to a dictionary) what the
idea involves, the cost of testing and/or of implementation, and what
the main benefits will be. A longer report attached should provide
the detailed background to which they can refer if they are sufficiently interested. Make it sharp and neatly packaged, and as tightly
tied to the company's overall growth objectives as you possibly
can.

You can help your own subordinates develop similar skills by forming internal task forces to find innovative solutions to departmental
problems. The more you can involve your people in the innovation
process, the more likely they are both to give rise to new ideas and
to accept the changes involved when some of those ideas are implemented. Indeed, when an unpalatable decision has to be made you
may find it useful to involve your subordinates in discussions, so that
they themselves can come up with the solution. They may have a better
idea than your original one. If they have only worse ideas, you can
then put yours forward and explain why it *is* better. If they have the
same idea as you, they will be obliged to commit themselves to it in

a manner that would not be possible if the same solution were imposed arbitrarily from above.

While monitoring the competition in general may not be your responsibility, you can be of great help to your company if you keep a close personal eye on what your counterparts in rival organizations are doing. You, after all, are more likely than anyone else to appreciate the significance of their actions. You will earn points for correctly assessing a competitor's intentions and helping to plan defensive innovation. At the same time, you may be able to detect weaknesses in the competitor not obvious to the marketing department, and help to design offensive innovations that will exploit them.

If you have a discretionary budget for trying out new ideas, do use it to the full. No one will respect you for saving it. If you haven't got a discretionary budget for this purpose, create one. You might, for example, hold back resources created by increased productivity and use them to invest people's time in trying or investigating novelties. As long as this activity is kept to a fairly small scale, it is unlikely to draw down wrath from above; but if it does, that is a fair indication that your company is not interested in encouraging innovation.

You can also improve your personal ability to innovate by:

- keeping up to date, not just with the literature in your immediate field, but also in parallel and emerging fields that might have some bearing on your work. For example, if you are in general engineering, you should have at least some knowledge of recent advances in electronics. If you are in advertising, you should have some interest in new methods of marketing, or in the development of new media. Many of the most significant product and process innovations come from applying and adapting ideas from one specialist area to another.

- establishing your own network for the exchange of information and ideas, whether or not the company has one already. This private network may give you a significant edge over other people in the company, and can be a useful source of tipoffs for interesting jobs elsewhere.

- joining and participating in professional institutions – especially if you are still under forty. The sad fact is that, while professional institutions can be a very effective means of keeping one's ear to the ground, most of the official positions tend to be taken up by a mixture of the great and the good, and of old buffers put out to grass. The institutional committees are usually desperately short of younger managers who are prepared to contribute action rather than words. These committees can provide you with the opportunity and resources legitimately to pursue innovative ideas which have been blocked within your company. At the same time, they give you a professional visibility that may prove very valuable in career terms. Beware, however, of letting them take up too much time that could be spent more usefully in your normal job.

FEW BARRIERS TO CHANGE

Time may not stay still, but most organizations need a lot of goading to keep up with it. We have already seen, in the chapter on 'Winning through autonomy', how important it is to maintain the small-company environment in large organizations, if they are to be able to react swiftly to external change. But even small operations can become ossified. If small automatically meant dynamic, the vast majority of small businesses would swiftly burgeon into major companies. In reality, of course, the opposite is true. Very few small companies are *consistently* innovative. Andrew Robertson asks pertinently: 'How many computer software companies have written *two* mould-breaking programs?'

Innovation has to be worked at to become consistent. It has to be driven hard, and the person at the wheel has to drive through or around obstacles along the way in the sure knowledge that the cargo behind is worth a few dents in the cab. Most of those obstacles will be inside rather than outside the company. Few organizations are short of people with ideas, and even if they are, ideas can be purchased relatively cheaply from outside. What is lacking is the ability to drive those ideas through the obstacle course to a successful product. An idea that may fit your company's objectives and strengths in every way may fail purely through lack of commitment.

The first step in removing the barriers to innovation is, rather obviously, identifying them. How many of the following barriers would you say typified your organization?

1. General attitudes towards innovation   US industrial psychologist Dr Mort Feinberg lists seven statements commonly to be heard in innovation resistant companies.

- 'Innovation is insubordination.' Instead of seeing suggestions of new ways of doing things as a genuine commitment to the organization's goals, managers see it as an attack on the established order.
- 'Why abandon a sure thing?' The cautious manager will always prefer to stick with something he knows to work, even if it doesn't work that well.
- 'We don't have the time or money to experiment.' That, says Feinberg, is 'merely a way of saying that the company gives a low priority to innovation'.
- 'A nice idea – but it's too ambitious.' Many managers badly underrate the resources at their disposal. Feinberg compares them with the gorilla, now an endangered species because it is unable to make good use of its powerful limbs and teeth and instinctively flees from danger.
- 'You're asking for trouble.' That's probably true, but it is also the nature of innovation, which rarely comes easy. The skill is to foresee and handle the problems that it will cause to the rest of the organization.
- 'He's upstaging the rest of us.' Also probably true, but who cares if the organization as a whole benefits?
- 'We tried it and it didn't work.' The most common copout of all, and almost never followed by 'because' and a rational explanation of why it didn't work. Just because an idea didn't work then, there is no reason to assume automatically that it will not work now. It may have been before its time and now be ripe for exploitation, with all the benefits of having encountered and mastered some of the bugs before. Or upon examination you may well find that it did not have a fair trial at all, that the dice were loaded against it from the start, but that now it really does merit a proper trial.

How many of those sound familiar to you?

2. **A poor risk/reward ratio** Sticking one's neck out to make suggestions or, even worse, to attempt to push through their execution against organizational resistance can be a very efficient form of corporate suicide in some organizations. Managers in these organizations tend to practise Mohr's Law ('Don't get any on you'); they listen to every idea with an ear tuned for flaws. If there is anything

at all wrong with an idea, they protect their backs by discarding it immediately without attempting to improve it. 'Do this well enough and often enough,' says Don Gamache, president of international innovation consultancy Innotech, 'and any potentially good ideas will *never* be presented.'

That clearly is an extreme. Yet it pays for every chief executive to examine regularly what the risk/reward ratio is for being an innovator. In particular, how does the reaction to the innovator's failure compare to that accorded to the conservative's inaction?

3. Lack of response and feedback on suggestions Every idea deserves acknowledgement, and it should be part of every manager's job to show publicly that he values the suggestions made by his subordinates. There doesn't have to be a physical reward involved, merely the knowledge that suggestions are useful and wanted. Even if the idea can't be used, it deserves a considered explanation of why. Too many company suggestion schemes provide stock answers to such ideas. After receiving two or three slips with the same wording, most people are likely to become discouraged. Although it requires considerably more effort, all suggestions ought to get an individual response.

Another common error is to delay too long before providing a reasoned response. One large multinational regularly takes six months to a year to respond to new product ideas from the field, while they go through various committees and in-trays. The message 'Proceed to investigate further' does not go down well to staff who are now trying to work out how to deal with the threat from a competitor who has implemented the same idea in the meantime.

4. Threat to job security Many of the most significant innovations at shopfloor level involve automation. Although resistance to automation is now starting to grow even in Japan, by and large Japanese companies have received remarkable co-operation from their employees in this process because those companies have guaranteed employment security. Scarcely any British companies have been prepared to offer employees such guarantees. Yet who in his right mind is going to innovate himself out of a job unless he knows he has another with equal or better pay and status lined up for him? Many excellent companies emphasize employment security rather than job security.

At Mitsubishi Motors, for example, the employees with the best record of generating productivity- and quality-oriented ideas are promoted to a select group. This group is supplied with all the equipment it needs to test promising ideas in a nearby area of the factory – and that is its sole task. Membership of the group is frequently a passport to management, so it is hardly surprising that ambitious young employees tend to look actively for workable suggestions. By contrast, a large British public-sector organization recently had to debate whether or not to praise an employee with a record number of successful suggestions on improving productivity, for fear that he would be accused of being a 'crawler'.

5. Rigid organizational structure   One of the benefits of matrix management (where the individual manager may report to more than one superior) is that it is more difficult to build up rigid barriers between departments. The more that managers of departments in the typical hierarchical organization feel they have to protect their patch, the more defensive they are going to be towards any innovation likely to result in fallout over their territory.

Knocking down these barriers frequently needs a sledgehammer and sometimes a bulldozer. Occasionally, very occasionally, people in the organization will accept the need for innovation so readily that the barrier collapses because its foundations have disintegrated – but don't count on that happening to you. Linking an element of incentive to overall company performance may help to bring in a more collaborative style.

Changing attitudes   is primarily a matter of leadership. Top management must put pressure on all departments to participate in the innovation process, and demand convincing reasons from those that don't.

If a department in your company fails to produce a flow of new ideas when asked to, it may be because the people there are lazy, because they are afraid of rejection, or because they don't know how. Of these, the easiest to deal with is the last. Fewer than half of European companies make use of even the most basic formal creativity techniques, and only a very small percentage use such techniques regularly as a matter of course. But most of them are easy to learn and to apply. While it may not be realistic to expect a wooden manager who has been in the same job for 15 years to turn into a dynamic lateral thinker overnight (although it has happened), any loosening up of people's thinking is a significant achievement.

If people are afraid of rejection, it may take more effort to change their attitude. Part of the answer lies in the changes in the internal environment, which we will deal with shortly. But a great deal can also be achieved simply by asking people for their suggestions on specific problems. Not by memo, or in a large group; but as individuals, face to face or at least by telephone. Few people can resist the flattery of being asked for help by someone senior. Moreover, under such circumstances they will pull out all the stops to be as creative as they can.

Of course, fear of rejection often stems from a previous bad experience. You don't normally stroke a dog that has already bitten you. Apart from reassuring people that he really does want suggestions, the more senior manager can make sure that they know how to present their ideas properly. As any venture capitalist, book publisher or producer of plays will confirm, it is the way in which ideas are presented that decides initially whether they get an adequate hearing. Training for innovation needs to include not only how to come up with ideas, but how to develop them and present them in a manner that allows more senior management to evaluate them swiftly and easily. We have been able to find very few companies that have a consistent policy to do this.

If the reason for lack of innovation is sheer laziness, then the problem is merely one of deciding the kind of pressures or sanctions to apply, with removal and replacement of particular individuals as one of the options.

Changing the risk/reward ratio requires considerable ground knowledge of people's feelings and beliefs. The rewards for successful innovation may be quite high and the penalties for failure quite low, but what counts is what people believe to be the case. Much can be done by simply stating and restating company policy, and publicizing cases where it has been put into effect. But to mount a truly effective campaign, the company needs to conduct what we might call a 'creativity audit'.

Such an audit first looks at where in the organization the new ideas are coming from. It does not matter whether these ideas are completely novel or borrowed from outside. What matters is that there is an unmistakable flow of innovation. The audit then compares the strength of the innovation flow in each area of the company with the strength needed to stay ahead of the competition in that respect (e.g. is marketing innovating as swiftly and as often as the best of the competition?). Finally, the audit examines the attitudes of people in those departments where the flow of innovation is inadequate.

Another useful source of information about attitudes towards the risks and rewards of innovation is to interview people leaving the company, and especially anyone leaving to set up his or her own business. Did they feel they could not establish a viable business within the company, and if so, why? Did the former employee who went to a competitor do so because no one would listen to his ideas in your company?

Armed with this information, it should normally be possible to create a risk/reward package that provides an adequate mixture of safeguards and attractions to make the majority of managers feel it is worthwhile sticking their necks out to pursue a good idea.

One element of such a package should be cash. 'There are only very few companies where the development of novel ideas and their successful implementation are duly integrated into the evaluation and reward system of senior managers,' complains Dr Rolf Berth of the International Management Institute (IMI) in Geneva. Yet the generation of successful ideas by a team of people is relatively easy to measure. (Measuring idea generation by individuals is more difficult, because everyone will lay claim to having had a part in a successful idea, and no one will admit dreaming up a bad one.)

Another element must be the acceptance by top management that failures are valuable for the lessons that can be learned from them. The company can establish the habit of conducting a post-mortem on all failures, with all the managers involved present. Intrinsic in the rules of the post-mortem is that there must be no apportionment of blame. Rather, the entire process must focus on the question: 'How can we *use* this experience?'

Lastly, the company must make a clear policy statement that organizational mavericks will be tolerated, indeed encouraged, under certain well-defined circumstances. In general, these will be in fast-moving new ventures, where the hot seat will be a high-risk one, but highly paid.

Improving response and feedback   It's surprising how few organizations have ever thought to measure the average time it takes a good idea to get from the bottom to the top. Those that do are frequently shocked. Obviously, the fewer management levels an idea has to go through for approval, the faster it will reach senior management. But even in fairly shallow hierarchies, there can be layers that slow things down: one level of management may have little else to do but filter and reorder information going up and down the chain. Alternatively, departmental management may be so busy handling day-to-day problems that is simply doesn't have time to pass ideas up the chain in a form that senior management can use, or only does so in an occasional desk-clearing binge. The result is that good ideas are either delayed or irretrievably lost in the system.

One solution is to impose a dual system of suggestions reporting. Employees at any level are encouraged to put their ideas down on a specially drafted form that asks most of the pertinent questions needed for more senior managers to make a first evaluation. One copy of the form is retained by the employee, another goes to his immediate superior, and a third bypasses the hierarchy to an innovation unit that reports directly to the chief executive. In this way, particularly promising ideas can be seized upon and hurried through the evaluation system by enquiry from the top.

The dual reporting system also means that promising ideas are not filtered out by some middle manager who does not appreciate their significance in top management's grand plan. As we have touched upon in the previous chapter, one of the primary reasons for lack of innovation by large companies is that so few usable ideas actually make their way to the top. As with the thousands of eggs in one frog's spawn, only two or three survive to hop on their own. The rest are eaten by a myriad of predators.

Removing the threat to job security The inability of most firms to find alternative employment for employees displaced by automation is only partly a matter of economics. Indeed, now that the drastic slimming process of the recession is over, it may be argued that the economic excuse for laying off labour is becoming much harder to justify. The top executive team that has its mind set firmly on growth ought to be able to absorb pretty well all the numbers whose jobs are now likely to be overtaken by automation. The reason why most firms fail to do so is that they are generally inept at manpower planning. They make lamentably little investment in training employees to be multi-skilled, and are often not prepared to be flexible over the jobs people can do.

Unless the company is prepared to make substantial commitments to its employees, it is unreasonable to expect them to make the commitment the company would like in terms of improving productivity. This is probably one reason why quality circles have in general been less enthusiastically received by British workforces than by Japanese, and, even where they have been implemented, frequently lose their edge after the most obvious suggestions have been made.

One important distinction that should be drawn here is between job security and employment security. Job security implies guaranteeing to people that the particular job they do will continue and that they can occupy it until they choose to leave, unless dismissed for cause. It can be seen in all its stultifying glory in the British national newspapers, where the inability to remove obsolete jobs has prevented employers from introducing modern technology and reduced the profitability of the whole industry to the point where most titles are at best marginally viable. Employment security means guaranteeing to people that, whatever happens to their particular tasks in the company, they can continue on the payroll. They may have to be retrained or transferred, but their monthly salary is secure.

You may not be able to offer employment security – nor may you want to, in the case of the worst employees – but you can go a long way towards making people feel secure. If you do have to let people go (the very phrase indicates just how unwilling senior management normally is to think about its policy on such matters until the crisis is upon it), the company should do so in a manner that minimizes recriminations. A substantial redundancy package, time off during working hours to seek another job, and 'outplacement' assistance in finding a suitable opening are all now standard in some of our largest companies. A few, such as ICI, now turned around under the leadership of John Harvey-Jones and an example of a company where the winning streak has been rekindled, go to exceptional lengths in this direction. ICI has an impressive portfolio of former employees it has funded in establishing their own businesses. The form this help takes varies, but typically it may be a guarantee of their salary over a period of one or two years, while the business gains its feet. It is, of course, easier to do this as the company becomes more profitable.

Programmes such as this are not aimed solely at the departing employee. They have at least as great an impact on those who remain, who recognize that the company will not simply cast them on the scrap heap as soon as they are no longer needed.

Adapting the organizational structure   to ease innovation is much easier said than done. After all, most organization structures were not designed with innovation as an objective. Quite the opposite, in fact: they have usually been designed to impose stability and order upon the various parts of the company.

Some practical suggestions, however, include:

● appoint someone at the highest management level as the 'innovation supremo' and ensure that he or she has resources and authority to intervene wherever internal barriers are preventing the flow of innovation

● prevent people from becoming stuck in the same functional rut by giving them relatively frequent job rotation. Even a specialist such as an economist or an accountant can benefit from a spell in a more generalist department such as marketing or personnel.

● make inter-disciplinary teams a fact of life in your company

● let the people who originate innovations move with them, even if that means going to another division

● create a formal procedure to allow organizational mavericks to operate as entrepreneurs, without the risk of their being sabotaged by less innovative managers who stick rigidly to the rule book

● establish a formal structure to evaluate and test ideas. This structure should be as swift-acting as possible. Another part of its franchise should be to review competitors' successful new ideas and why it was that they got there first.

What the individual manager can do   You have both a support role and a personal role to play in the innovation stakes. You have a responsibility to innovate within the guidelines top management sets, and to facilitate the generation of ideas by your subordinates.

Start first with yourself. How many of the excuses for not innovating do you habitually use? Experiment by running an ideas generating session with your subordinates and tape-recording the discussion. Analyse your reactions to their ideas. How many did you dismiss and what reasons did you give? You may well find that, however positive you intended to be, your language gives others a very negative impression.

Make sure that your behaviour doesn't push the risk/rewards ratio the wrong way. Do you jump on people who use their initiative?

Ask your subordinates bluntly whether they feel you want them to come up with ideas. If a subordinate's bright idea does not work, never abandon him to the wolves – not unless you wish to condition him to keep his bright ideas to himself in future. Protect him by taking the blame yourself, if necessary. The gesture is unlikely to cost you much, but is sure to be noticed both above and below.

Make sure that you respond to all ideas swiftly, but not instantaneously. Don't necessarily give an off-the-cuff reply; that can appear dismissive if you have to say no. Moreover, you may on reflection discover merits in the idea that were not immediately obvious. It's much harder to rekindle enthusiasm after you have dowsed it than if you have kept it warm.

Develop your listening skills, so that you can work with subordinates to turn promising ideas into good ideas. The more people see that you are willing to spend time with them on their ideas, the more ideas they will bring to you. You cannot provide guarantees of employment (you are just as much in top management's hands as your subordinates are) but you can do a great deal to make sure that people who report to you are all trained in a sufficiently wide range of skills to improve the chances of the company being able to make use of them elsewhere. One way of doing so is to organize your department so that everyone gets the maximum opportunity to learn a number of skills rather than just one.

NATURAL CURIOSITY ABOUT HOW THINGS ARE DONE ELSEWHERE

What the chief executive can do   Knowing what the competition is up to or is likely to be up to is an essential part of the formulation of strategy. It is also usually very badly done. An even better reason for keeping a close eye on the competition is what you can learn from them. If they are doing something – anything – better than you are, then in the name of excellence you have little choice but to determine why, how and whether you could do it better still.

The innovation-minded company will not look just within its own market or industry for examples to adopt and adapt, however. It recognizes that good ideas occur in the most unlikely places. The trick is to be open to such ideas and to recognize how they could be applied to your company. As Theodore Levitt once pointed out, 'Information only yields meaning with imagination.' That said, it is depressing how little use most companies make of the information resources readily available to them. For example, how many consumer goods manufacturers make use of services that monitor the products put on to the shelves of stores in other countries?

The message is rammed home once again by comparison with the Japanese, who, while not quite the paragons of industrial excellence suggested in so much of the management literature in recent years, do have some good practices to pass on. A recent comparative study of how Japanese and US companies monitor technical developments in each other's countries found that the Japanese were far more thorough. The US research managers relied for most their information on Japanese developments on translated technical papers and digests, many of them two to three years old before they were published in English. The technical data bases the US managers relied upon to tip them off about new developments turned out to contain only 25 per cent of the relevant Japanese patents.

The Japanese conducted their technological monitoring in a far more systematic way, through a variety of specialized agencies such as the Japan Information Center for Science and Technology, and managed to catch virtually all the important developments in their fields. Most of the US firms thought they were doing a much more competent job of monitoring developments than they actually were, and had little idea of the amount of R&D being done by Japanese firms in their fields. Were a similar study to be undertaken in Britain, much the same results might be expected.

You can help to ensure that your company maintains high natural curiosity by:

● making other company's good ideas known in your organization. Most companies are very coy about openly discussing the achievements of other companies, and paranoiac about discussing those of direct competitors. But what better way to educate employees about the need to innovate than showing them what they are up against?

● attending and/or sponsoring conferences and seminars on topics at the edge of the company's mainstream interests

● joining in relevant collaborative research projects with companies outside your normal markets

● encouraging employees to visit other companies, where they may pick up good ideas

What the individual manager can do Take time out to look at yourself objectively. Are your work interests broadly or narrowly based? A simple test may be to look at the reading matter that passes over your desk. How much of it is internally generated and how much of it external? Do the magazines you read all relate to your specialization, or do you scan a wider range of publications? The fact is that few, if any, innovations are plucked from thin air. They emerge from juxtapositions of other ideas. The wider you spread your net for ideas, the more likely you are to catch something really useful.

You can improve your personal ability to innovate by:

● keeping up to date with the literature in your own and other fields
● establishing your own network to exchange information and ideas
● joining and participating in professional institutions

INTERNATIONAL PERSPECTIVE

What the chief executive can do Foreign travel is not a luxury in today's business climate; it's a necessity, if only as a means of knowing the enemy. Firms in Japan make a practice of sending all promising young managers to work abroad for at least two years. The idea is to give them a permanent international perspective on their markets.

Most British companies are trying desperately to reduce the number of employees they send to work abroad. There are good reasons for doing so, including the cost of maintaining expatriate staff, the desire of developing nations to install locals in management posts, and the dismal experiences many British companies have had after appointing expatriates to run US acquisitions.

Yet unless British companies learn to produce a generation of managers with international experience, they will continue to be handicapped in international markets. One possible solution is to increase the rate at which people are exchanged between subsidiaries around the world on temporary secondment. To do that, of course, the company needs to have sufficient overseas units. While these will normally be for local sales, manufacture or service, there is a growing recognition among some firms that having operations in, say, the United States and Japan has subtler, potentially more valuable benefits. Not only are units in both countries superb testing grounds for new products, but they are essential eyes and ears searching for new technologies that may be either a threat or an opportunity for the domestic business.

International trade tours tend to be disparaged by many companies as expensive 'showing the flag' exercises. And that is just what they are likely to be, unless the company spends considerable care and effort in preparing them. There has to be a clear itinerary, not merely of government officials and companies to sell to, but of people to learn from. For the Japanese, the primary purpose of a trade mission is business intelligence gathering, in its broadest sense.

You can create this international perspective by:

● the amount of travel you and your top management colleagues do. If you spend all your time with the domestic operations, it is a clear sign that you do not consider the overseas dimension of the business to be important.

● the ease with which you permit international travel. While every trip must be justified to prevent people disappearing on costly junkets, you can remove much of the red tape required to gain permission to travel. Indeed, you might consider international exposure to be so important for key managers that you demand an explanation if they have *not* made a justifiable trip abroad within a reasonable period.

● the value you place upon ideas from abroad, as disclosed in internal company communications. Don't be afraid to stress the origin of a new product or process: the fact that it has already worked in, say, the United States or West Germany is likely to increase people's faith in its chances here.

What the individual manager can do   If you can travel, do. Take at least one or two opportunities a year to visit overseas plants or to attend international symposia. When there, take every opportunity you can to pick up new ideas.

In terms of ideas gathering, some of the real professionals are feature journalists. The best of them extract the most from conferences by:

- ignoring the formal speeches. They are almost always printed out and can be read in comfort later. Even the questions and answers (which they normally do listen to) can often be purchased on audio cassette shortly afterwards.
- attending the informal side-sessions, where people ask and answer questions in a more relaxed, unguarded manner
- circulating among as many people as possible during morning, afternoon and lunchtime breaks

DIRECTED R&D

What the chief executive can do   The successful companies in *The Winning Streak* all ensured that their research and development efforts were closely concentrated around definable market objectives, and that people in the R&D department understood those objectives. Most of them also integrated R&D into the organization in a manner which obliged other departments involved in the implementation of the new product or process idea (production, finance, marketing, sales and so on) to commit themselves to it at an early stage.

Gordon Edge, chief executive of PA Technology, has been looking at this issue for many years. His advice on achieving similar mechanisms in your company can be summarized as follows:

Clearly drawn commercial constraints are actually a help to scientific creativity, because they give it direction – so much so that they become the foundation stone of innovation rather than its boundary. It is the presence of clear and perhaps tough commercial goals that focuses the R&D team's thinking. Not only must the interaction between R&D and marketing be close, with R&D having a clear understanding of marketing objectives, but good communications between R&D and all other departments are essential. The complexities of managing in the modern world dictate that there must be a variety of specializations, such as finance, personnel, production, maintenance and so on, all of which build their functional barriers around themselves. Yet the national cultures, such as the United States, Japan and West Germany, which are on average more successful at swift implementation of good ideas commonly overlay their multi-disciplinary structure with an inter-disciplinary structure, where marketing, product planning, finance and R&D create and implement strategy together.

In other words, technological innovation cannot be left to the R&D department alone. Companies that practice this inter-disciplinary management of new product development typically place the project in the hands of a project manager, who brings in other people from the various departments at appropriate stages of development. Marketing and finance will normally be represented from the beginning, however, rather than brought in at the last moment and asked to give their sanction and commitment to a product in whose development and conception they have had little or no influence.

Two other points made by Edge concern the physical side of R&D. Firstly, most R&D departments are designed for anything but creative interaction. Locked away in separate laboratories, it is not unknown for two teams in some of the largest R&D establishments to be working on the same problem, each unaware of what the other is doing. When US conglomerate TRW (which has invested a remarkable amount of time and effort in ensuring that technology is disseminated rapidly and thoroughly throughout its many subsidiaries) made a study of software productivity, it found that a very high proportion of the work had already been done somewhere else in the group. Most companies just aren't aware of how much time they waste reinventing the wheel.

TRW's solution to its software problem was to automate the writing of new software in such a way that it would always be possible to pull out any existing programs that covered the same or similar ground. Edge's more general solution is to design laboratories so that they encourage inter-disciplinary interaction between research teams. At the same time, if teams are set up around projects, rather than as specialist centres of expertise that handle a number of projects at one time, there will be a constant movement of people and rubbing off of ideas.

Edge's second point relates to the funding of R&D. Today's R&D department needs a champion at top management level, if only to obtain the cash to equip its laboratories properly. The capital investment for the average R&D employee in the UK has fallen way behind that for his counterpart in, say, West Germany or the United States. While R&D capital investment is often more difficult to justify in terms of productivity or direct returns, it is none the less essential if the company is serious about competing internationally (or domestically, for that matter, because if you don't go for the competition, sooner or later they'll come for you).

One of the truisms of advertising is that the best time to spend heavily is during a market downturn, when more short-sighted companies are cutting back on their advertising expenditure. The same general principle applies to R&D. In a series of studies made by one of the authors for *Chief Executive* magazine into how various industry sectors were faring after the recession of the late 1970s and early 1980s, it became clear that those now in the strongest market positions tended to be the companies which had maintained or even increased the level of their investment in R&D during the difficult period. In almost every case, this controversial decision had been made and held to by the chief executive.

What the individual manager can do   In the chapter on 'Winning through market orientation', we look briefly at how the research and development manager can bring the marketing perspective to bear on his department's activities. The other side of the coin, of course, is how managers elsewhere in the firm can make use of the R&D perspective in identifying opportunities for useful innovation.

In order to do that, you must have at least a basic idea of what scientific and technological resources are available to your company. If you have labs and haven't toured them, do. Whether your company has labs or not, you should build up enough technological literacy to understand what the new technologies can do. At the minimum you should attend a computer awareness course and scan popular science magazines such as *New Scientist* and the British Association's *Link-up*, the 'Innovation' page of the *Sunday Times* and the technology page of the *Financial Times*. Even if you never come up with an applicable idea from any of these sources you will at least be building a useful vocabulary that will enable you to discuss these issues with more senior managers – and that in itself is worth a few points in the management survival game.

THE ROLE OF THE CHIEF EXECUTIVE

The question in this chapter about the amount of time the chief executive spends on innovation is highly pertinent. IMI's Berth puts it succinctly:

Managers in general and board members in particular have the tendency to underline their love for creative innovations at after-dinner speeches and at annual meetings. But when it comes to true decision making that deep love falters somewhat; and if we look at various surveys which have tried to pinpoint how top managers spend their time, it becomes evident that the hours devoted to the management of change are few. It mostly falls short of the 20 to 25 per cent which many authors and consultants feel adequate. This is particularly disquieting as innovation and the establishment of an innovative culture are two tasks which can least stand delegation. Unless those with general responsibility personally devote time and effort to innovation, there is little hope that the normally underestimated creative potential of people can be released.

There is indeed a great difference between using innovation as a pleasant filler for pep talks and actually *living* innovation as a critical part of the organization's strategy. Of all the themes top management should stress when it is stomping round the outposts of the corporate empire, the need for and reasons behind change are likely to strike the strongest chords. Change is, by its very nature, unsettling, even if we are fully aware of what will happen. The less sure people are of the outcome, the more likely they are to resist, overtly or covertly.

At the same time, top management can make a practice of commenting on specific innovations rather than innovation in general. In touring round the offices or the laboratories, the chief executive and his colleagues should ensure that they ask informed questions, discuss why a project has been tackled in a particular way and, if possible, suggest improvements to the idea or other sources of expertise elsewhere that the employees concerned might tap. Try hard to understand what people at the sharp end are doing. The objective of this involvement in the detail of innovation is not to influence the outcome directly. It is to establish that top management truly is interested in innovation and is not simply paying lip service to the concept.

We looked earlier in this chapter at ways to bypass the normal slow channels through which innovative ideas ascend the corporate hierarchy. By singling out individual ideas with particular promise and talking them over with the employee concerned, the chief executive can virtually guarantee a constant flood of suggestions from that part of the company for months afterwards. It all goes to show that, if the chief executive genuinely wants innovation and is prepared to show that he wants it, sooner or later he will have all he can handle.

In those companies that win consistently on the international stage, innovation almost always turns out to be the responsibility of the chief executive himself. Even in those few cases where there is a board member responsible for innovation, the chief executive maintains a high profile in that area, to demonstrate how important he considers it to be.

Another ingredient these winning companies have is the ability to put their innovation strategies into practice. Again, this will only happen with a direct and positive involvement and commitment by the chief executive himself.

What the individual manager can do   If you aim to become a chief executive yourself, now is the time to practise being an innovation leader. Most of the behaviour and attitudes required of the chief executive if he is to make innovation count throughout the organization can be learnt early on. All you need to make them habitual is commitment now.

8 Winning through integrity

Do people feel that your company is 'good to do business with'? Do they feel it is trustworthy and well-intentioned or tricky, hard-nosed and interested solely in maximizing short-term profits?

Corporate values that last and count have one thing in common: they are all things most people can respect. If people respect your company's values, they are likely to respect the company. If they respect the company, they are more likely to buy from it than from a competitor they respect less. It may seem a long chain of cause and effect, but it works.

In *The Winning Streak* we referred to this phenomenon as integrity. You might prefer to call it trust, or fair dealing. Whatever word you use, the moral is the same: companies that are successful in the long term establish relationships with all the people they deal with – customers, suppliers, employees and the public at large – based on absolute honesty and mutual respect. 'Of course we conduct our business honestly,' you may say. But does your company embrace integrity as an integral part of its philosophy? Does it simply hope that employees will deal fairly with the public or suppliers, or does it actively go out of its way to *make sure* that they do? The following questions will help you establish whether integrity is a way of life in your company.

GENERAL QUESTIONS

1 Does your company have . . .?

> *a statement of its moral philosophy*
> *a policy for social responsibility*

2 Does your company respond to a slur on its integrity with . . .?

*an immediate defence and an invitation to the detractors to take a
proper look for themselves
an angry denial and consultation with the lawyers
ignoring it/treating it with the contempt it deserves*

INTEGRITY TOWARDS EMPLOYEES

3 How accurately do you know your company's opinion of your
performance and your prospects?

*very well
partially
no idea*

4 Do people in your company get visible credit for a job well done
and a private ticking off for a job badly done?

5 When visiting top management holds 'informal' meetings with
the troops, can you ...?

*ask anything you feel important and know you will get a frank
answer
ask anything you like but know you might not get a frank answer
ask anything you like as long as it won't offend
ask anything you like as long as it's about the weather*

6 Does your company believe that ...?

*once it has hired someone, it has a responsibility to do all it can to
retain them in employment
employees are responsible for their own future; the company's responsibility ends when the legal notice runs out*

7 Is there a specific feedback system that makes sure that top management *knows* whether employees are receiving fair treatment?

8 How often do official company documents mention the word 'loyalty'?

*frequently
occasionally
never*

INTEGRITY TOWARDS SUPPLIERS

9a   When did your company last ask its suppliers what they thought of it?

> *within the past year*
> *within the past two years*
> *within the past five years*
> *who cares?*

b   If your company has asked them, do they rate it as...?

> *fairer than the competition*
> *as fair as the competition*
> *less fair than the competition*

c   Would the suppliers' attitude to your company best be described as...?

> *friendly*
> *respectful*
> *suspicious*
> *thorough dislike*

10   Does your company always choose the supplier who offers the best value for money?

11a   How far does your company involve its suppliers in its long-term plans?

> *intimately: the better they can plan, the more likely we can fulfil our plans*
> *occasionally, on a 'need to know' basis*
> *only when we have to*

b   Do they ask your company's advice on long-term plans before making major investments in plant or labour?

12   A long-term supplier runs into difficulties. Would your company...?

> *look for ways to bail it out*
> *take no action*
> *pull out and find another supplier before the ship sinks*

13 In making payments to suppliers does your company . . .?

take into account the supplier's needs
pay promptly as a matter of course
keep the cash till the last possible moment

14 Does your company look out for new product opportunities for long-term suppliers?

15 Does your company establish clear standards for its suppliers' general integrity and behaviour as well as for the quality of goods and services?

16 A major supplier to your company is revealed to have an appalling record in its employment practices in an overseas subsidiary. Would your company . . .?

suggest quietly to the chairman of that company that this could affect the business relationship between your two companies
cut that company off immediately
decide it's none of your business

17 How often does your secretary lie to suppliers about your availability?

never
occasionally
frequently

INTEGRITY TOWARDS THE CUSTOMER

18 Can you honestly say your company is completely fair to its customers?

19 How well does the picture in your company's report and accounts fit reality?

completely
fairly well
not very well
hardly at all

20 How often does the phrase 'value for money' appear in your company's internal memos?

> *frequently*
> *rarely*
> *never*

21 An internal study reveals that one of your company's products has a design fault. Do you ...?

> *inform all users immediately and offer to put it right*
> *keep quiet until the first articles appear in the Press*
> *refuse to admit it publicly at all*

INTEGRITY TOWARDS THE PUBLIC IN GENERAL

22 Your company is informed it is in contravention of pollution control legislation. Does top management ...?

> *initiate action to look at the whole problem with a view to possibly exceeding the legal requirements*
> *do what it has to to meet the requirements*
> *do what it can to get round the requirements*

23 How good are your company's relations with the local authority?

> *very good*
> *quite good*
> *indifferent*
> *atrocious*

24 Has your company ever asked its residential neighbours what they think of it?

25 Would you like to live next door to one of your company's plants?

26 When was the last time your unit of the company had a public open day?

> *within the past year*

> *within the past three years*
> *longer than three years ago*
> *never*

27 What is your company's relationship with environmental and other public pressure groups?

> *generally good*
> *indifferent*
> *cold war*
> *open war*

28 Has any employee of your company ever 'blown the whistle' on activities that would be publicly disapproved of?

POINTS TO WATCH:

Question **9c** – You are not in business to win popularity contests. If they actually like you, you probably pay too much, too soon. Respect is far more businesslike.

Question **10** – It is tempting to answer yes here. But consider which is more valuable in the long term: a stable relationship with a supplier who values your custom and understands your needs, or *ad hoc* suppliers, none of whom have any special loyalty to your company?

Question **13** – If you chose 'pay promptly', think again. Not everybody *needs* swift payment, and there are enough deliberately slow-paying companies to put you at a disadvantage if you treat all suppliers with the same generosity. On the other hand some suppliers (especially fledgeling small businesses) really do need swift payment and will be much more loyal to you if they receive it. It can, in fact, be worthwhile paying these companies in less than 30 days.

GENERAL POINTS

What the chief executive can do An organization's moral tone comes more than anything else from how people perceive top management. It is not that people expect their leaders to be paragons of virtue in all respects (indeed, they tend to be suspicious of the person who appears to be too perfect); but they do look to top management for a lead in the things that matter in business. If people who deal directly with the customer see the chief executive of their company as sharp and unscrupulous, they are likely to adopt some of the same attitudes towards the customer. Similarly, the more middle and junior management regard top management attitudes as unethical, the more likely they are to take a relatively cavalier approach to their relationships with employees, suppliers and the public in general.

That is why it is important for you as chief executive deliberately to set the tone of morality you want to see operate in your company. You can do this in a number of ways, including:

● examine your business behaviour and your reputation in the City and elsewhere. Do people outside and inside the firm believe that you apply high ethical standards to your business dealings? If they don't, you have a problem with either your image, or your actual behaviour, or both. Changing the image is partly a matter of public relations, but is unlikely to be very effective if the reality behind it does not improve. Changing your behaviour, however, is like giving up smoking: you can become very accomplished at giving up, because you have so much practice. This, of course, defeats the whole object of the exercise, because integrity by definition is constant and consistent. The only sure way, apart from a massive application of willpower, is to determine a company code of ethics and enlist the help of your top management colleagues in making sure that you (and they) stick to it rigidly. All decisions you make should be measured against the code. Above all, give a copy to your personal secretary and your spouse, and explain the thinking behind it. Encourage them, too, to speak up if an action or decision seems to go against the spirit of the code. Remember: your best critics are those closest to you.

● distribute the code in writing to every employee in the company, and encourage every manager to discuss it with his subordinates in a cascade briefing. Make sure the code is included in your company's induction literature. If people don't know and understand the thinking behind the code of behaviour, it becomes difficult to rap them over the knuckles for not sticking to it.

- use the various company communications to provide examples of the code in action. For example, why the decision was made to walk away from a particular deal or how a problem of health and safety was foreseen and overcome. Stress the ethical implications behind such decisions enough, and eventually people will begin to accept that they, too, are bound by the code.
- react swiftly, firmly and openly when breaches of the code occur. If you turn a blind eye even to relatively minor infractions, you are effectively saying that the ethical issues are not important. You do not have to be draconian in your reactions. But you do have to demonstrate that you mean what you say and that you will not tolerate actions that might bring your company's reputation into disrepute.
- conduct a periodic review, preferably through an external observer (perhaps a non-executive director with the specific brief to act as ethical adviser) of the functioning of ethics within your company. Publish his review, warts and all, either in full or in a condensed version in the annual report. Don't be afraid that this will provide ammunition for ill-wishers to use against your company. Your openness in admitting the company is not perfect, but that you are constantly working towards improvement in its social responsibility, is a very good defence. It is very difficult for anyone to attack without appearing to hinder your attempts at improvement.

If it does happen that your company does come under attack for what a group in society considers to be immoral or unethical behaviour, do you already know how you would react? In our experience, most chief executives refuse to countenance this possibility until it actually happens. Only when a pressure group buys a handful of shares and asks awkward questions at the annual general meeting do they even begin to take the issues seriously. Any response is likely to be hastily conceived and defensive rather than well-researched and open, and this, of course, leads to frustration on both sides.

Yet it is as important for you to defend the company honour properly as it is to mount an adequate defence against predatory competition. Any attack on the company's ethics affects public trust, which in turn hits share prices, changes purchasing decisions and reduces people's willingness to make word of mouth recommendations.

The companies described in *The Winning Streak* have not been immune to such attacks. Marks & Spencer suffered a heated row at an annual general meeting a few years ago over what some shareholders regarded as unacceptable directors' perks; housebuilders Barratt Holdings were under fire as we completed that book; and as we write now cleaning contractors Pritchard are being taken to task for the allegedly low pay scales of their South African subsidiary. None of them can be said to have handled the matter well – which is yet another argument for putting considerable effort into avoiding the problem in the first place. You can improve your company's handling of such issues in the following ways:

● take on board the concept of issues management, i.e. the identification of socially contentious issues and the development of a corporate policy and approach to them.

● take executive responsibility for the company's good name yourself. Even if you have a public affairs director, he or she will not normally have the clout within the company to insist that other departments adopt different policies or behaviour. You wouldn't normally consider delegating responsibility for your own good name to anyone else, would you? To many people inside and outside the organization, you *are* the company, especially if you are the founder or majority shareholder.

● if you do come under fire for ethical reasons, try to look at it from the pressure group's point of view. Why have these people come to the conclusion they have? What fundamentally different belief do they have that makes them interpret the facts differently? Do they indeed have all the facts?

Do enter into dialogue, but maintain that dialogue on an ethical plane. Take the issue of South African involvement, simply because it occurs so frequently. If you strongly believe that your company has a moral responsibility not to desert its employees there, express your argument in those terms. Introduce the protesters and dissenters to some of the employees there, via video, and help them to see your moral dilemma. Most criticism comes because outsiders assume you are taking an immoral or amoral stance. If they perceive that your actions are taken upon ethical grounds, you will at least have gained their understanding, and may well also have convinced them that the issue is not as clear-cut as they had considered. In exceptional circumstances, you may even convince them that your view is correct.

In such circumstances, you must also be open and willing to listen to what they have to say. The most common complaint of public pressure groups about their meetings with top management is that 'They were only meeting us out of politeness. They weren't really interested in our point of view. They just wanted to justify their own. We never got on to the same wavelength.' It is probably unreasonable to expect the representatives of the pressure group to understand the intricacies of business management at corporate level. Therefore, if you aim to have a meaningful dialogue, you must switch to their wavelength. In presenting your problems in their terms, you will not only gain greater mutual understanding, but you may also receive practical suggestions on how to deal with the issue in a way that will satisfy both social and profit objectives. Asking them to put themselves in your shoes shares the ethical responsibility. If they cannot come up with a better answer than your own, their ability to criticize your company's behaviour is greatly blunted, even if they cannot bring themselves to give open support.

What the individual manager can do   Whether you recognize it at the time or not, how you feel about the company you work for affects your behaviour. If you want to develop good, ethical habits, choose your employer by his reputation for integrity. Ask customers and suppliers how they feel about the company and its behaviour in the marketplace. Look at the annual report: does it give an impression of openness or of secrecy? Run a quick search through one of the Press libraries for newspaper and magazine comment on the company: is the overall impression one of a company in business for the long term, determined to build up long-lasting relationships with employees, customers and suppliers, or does it appear to be on the make?

Working for a company with a poor public reputation can affect your personal value in the jobs market. If your company is known for sailing close to the wind, it can put you at a competitive disadvantage as a candidate for jobs in more reputable companies. It is automatically assumed that some of the previous company's dubious values will have rubbed off on you, and the longer you stay, the more tarnished you will be assumed to be. Protesting your innocence will make you seem like a used-car salesman trying to appear shy and sensitive.

The only circumstance under which you should consider remaining in an organization with a dubious reputation is when a 'new broom' chief executive makes clear his intention of changing the corporate ethos. As long as he lasts, there exist significant opportunities for bright, committed managers to help in the building up of a very different organization. Respond to the new chief executive's initiative by taking an initiative of your own. Write to him, letting him know how pleased you are at the change in attitude and asking if there is a role for you on any task force he may set up to bring about ethical change. Send a copy to your immediate superior. This approach both establishes you as a right-minded individual conscious of the corporate good and gives you valuable exposure at the highest level. If the new chief executive proves too much of a burr to the board and is fired, that is a good time for you too to look elsewhere. You will, after all, be taking with you ethical credentials that give you as an individual a competitive advantage even though your former company's reputation is still doubtful.

INTEGRITY TOWARDS EMPLOYEES

What the chief executive can do   Why is it that some managers can be autocratic, hard-nosed and unpleasant, yet still receive respect and commitment from their subordinates? The answer seems to be that these managers always make sure that people know where they stand. If a person is doing well, they will tell him so, often publicly. If someone is doing badly, they will also tell him or her so, bluntly and with little or no attempt to soften the blow. They are also consistent in the reasons for their praise and disapproval. By contrast, the 'nice guy' manager frequently cannot bring himself to tell someone his or her work is terrible. He allows weaknesses to continue, in the hope that they will get better of their own accord. Inevitably some simply fester until what was a minor problem for an employee becomes a major performance issue that puts his job in jeopardy. The 'nice guy' manager also sometimes finds himself backed into a corner where he has to act tough. Being unused to the role, he tends to ham it up. The inconsistency of his approach unsettles his subordinated, who never quite know where they are with him.

Most people don't live too well with uncertainty. They prefer to be told exactly what their employer thinks of them, even if the opinion is unpalatable. At least then they know what they have to do to improve. As a rule, the greatest motivation comes from making praise public and making dressings-down private, but however the company handles such situations, employees should always be given a full and accurate picture of their relationship to the company.

Making sure that this happens is a matter of management style. While performance appraisals can help, they are at best a six-monthly exercise. What employees actually need is a day-to-day appreciation of their performance. Telling someone they could have done better in something completed and forgotten several months ago is not particularly helpful. The best time to register satisfaction or dissatisfaction is straight away.

You can create that management style first by exhibiting it yourself, then by insisting that all managers build it into their daily routines. Your visits to plants and offices give an ideal opportunity to demonstrate what you mean by talking straight. When employees ask questions give them the blunt, truthful answer, not the answer you think they would like to hear. If you create a reputation as an open-speaking guy with no tolerance for bullshit, managers down the line will be put under increasing pressure from their subordinates to be similarly forthright. You will probably have to institute some form of group training for 'nice guy' managers, perhaps creating peer groups where they can offer each other mutual support in tackling unpleasant duties. With experience, most people learn how to be cruel to be kind.

Alongside honesty to employees lies fairness. It's not enough simply to expect all employees to be treated fairly. You have to make sure that they are being treated fairly, and that they can see that this is so. You must have some method of ensuring that unfairness is exposed. In those cases that come to your attention you must be prepared to intervene publicly, both to put matters right and to demonstrate the importance you attach to ensuring that everyone has a fair deal in your company.

In the end, the relationship between the company and the employee is one of loyalty. You expect a degree of loyalty *from* employees; yet how much effort do you put into ensuring that the company shows loyalty *to* the employees? The issue of loyalty is rarely discussed except in the breach (for example, when an executive quits, taking several key customers with him), and almost never in relation to the company's responsibilities. Yet it is patently unrealistic to expect loyalty to be one-sided.

If you wish to grow loyalty within your company you can:

● make sure that everyone recognizes the mutual nature of the relationship
● accept that it places obligations on the company as well. One of those obligations is to take at least some responsibility for finding alternative employment for those employees who, through no fault of their own, become redundant.
● establish policies that reward loyalty – for example, special share options after so many years of service

What the individual manager can do   Do your subordinates regard you as being straight with them? Do you prevaricate over a difficult issue, or tell it like it is? Is the treatment you mete out the same to all subordinates or do you have favourites? Do you play political games with your subordinates, 'to keep them on their toes'? Do you like to see people off balance?

You probably won't be able to answer those questions yourself. Ask your peers and your subordinates, and anyone else who may regularly observe your behaviour. If the picture that emerges is not one of consistent openness and fairness, you can begin to change your behaviour by making a weekly review of your interactions with your subordinates. Simply write down all the major events of the week that involved subordinates. Ask yourself 'Was there anything I could have told them that I didn't?' 'Was turning down John's application to go on a course consistent with accepting Christine's?' 'Was Peter completely to blame for losing that order?' If you have significant doubt, err on the side of the employee.

The more your subordinates know where they stand with you, the easier you will find it to build a cohesive, relaxed and committed team.

INTEGRITY TOWARDS SUPPLIERS

What the chief executive can do   Do you know how your suppliers rate your company as compared to its competitors? It is surprising how few chief executives have ever even thought of finding out. Yet the extra goodwill you may gain from having a better relationship may provide a significant competitive edge in, for example, speed of delivery or willingness to handle a special order. The principles of market research can be applied just as easily to suppliers. What you learn may cause you to make radical changes in how you organize your purchasing and supply operations.

Just as you want your customers to be with you for the long term, so you should aim to establish long-term relationships with suppliers – not least because it stabilizes the supply chain, allowing you to concentrate on improving the effectiveness and efficiency of the chain as a whole rather than link by link.

This long-term perspective also requires you to consider how your company can help them to develop to your advantage. Get involved in their development, but don't overload them by taking up too much of their capacity. Actively encourage them to seek other, preferably non-competitive markets for their products. Help them with current or future problems. Make them part of the family.

As with employees, you should have very strict but consistent requirements and make sure they understand them. Suppliers respect consistency, even if the standard demanded is exceptionally high. They do not respect inconsistency, which is far more difficult, time-consuming and costly for them to deal with.

One way of gaining a different and useful perspective on suppliers is to turn the supply chain on its head and view them as customers. What would a customer think if you continually tweaked up the price on spurious excuses, or changed the specifications of the product without telling him until just before delivery? He probably would not buy from you again. Yet many firms think nothing of comparable behaviour towards suppliers. Ask yourself 'If I were a supplier to this company, would it be because I *had* to do business with it or because I *wanted* to do business with it?' If you have to admit that your company is a poor customer, you should begin to look at how you can create a more positive relationship with your suppliers, based on mutual growth and profitability.

What the individual manager can do   Become the champion of your suppliers. Work with them. Help make sure their bills get paid, by checking personally with the accounts department. Be straight with them: let them into your plans, advise them on how to grow, on new opportunities opening up inside or outside your company that you are aware of. Make them feel their services or products are respected and valued. Put yourself in their shoes: would having to make twenty phone calls to get an overdue bill paid make you respect the company more or less? Do they feel they can rely on your word? How often have you been obliged to let them down, going back on a verbal agreement or promise?

In building up a relationship of trust and mutual confidence with your suppliers you are doing more than enhancing the company's reputation. You are enhancing your own.

INTEGRITY TOWARDS THE CUSTOMER

What the chief executive can do   Draw up a customer's charter. For example: The customer who buys from us has a right to expect:

- good value for money
- courteous, friendly service
- as safe and durable a product as is possible to provide
- complete honesty in all advertising and promotional materials
- to receive what he pays for (e.g. no big boxes with small contents)

If you want your customers still to be your customers in fifty years' time, you have to give them good reasons for sticking with you.

Just having a pious statement of intent is no more than a starting point. You have to make sure that those values are reflected in everything that happens within the company. That can be a tall order. While Sir John Sainsbury can personally test hundreds of grocery and household products a year, it is rather more difficult for the chief executive of a machine tool or aircraft manufacturer to check the quality of his company's products. He has to rely on information from a lot of other people, some of whom may have a vested interest in keeping the bad points about the product away from his notice.

One way or another, you need some form of semi-independent organization which can monitor whether the customer's charter is being held to. This should probably not be the customer relations department, which normally does not have sufficient authority to enforce change. The person responsible must be at board level. One company that has created an interesting model to follow is Gillette Co, which has appointed a vice president for product integrity, with authority to pull any product off the shelves at any time if it fails to meet the standards a consumer would expect. Products that have been withdrawn as a result include a line of batteries shown to present a possible health hazard, and an aerosol can that delivered only three-quarters of its contents. The product integrity department also examines the products of all potential acquisition candidates to ensure that they meet Gillette's exacting standards; a number of otherwise promising acquisition deals have folded as a result of its reports.

It takes courage to take such decisive action. But then integrity is all about having high principles and the guts to stick to them.

What the individual manager can do   Most departments interface with the customers in some way. Accounts, for example, can have a significant effect on customer relations by the quality and tone of the invoices it sends out. From time to time, put yourself in the shoes of a customer receiving service at the hands of your department and ask 'How would I feel about this company if I were one of its customers?' Use the answers to make changes in your department's practices and policies. The more direct and frequent your department's interaction with the customers, the more often you should repeat the exercise.

INTEGRITY TOWARDS THE PUBLIC IN GENERAL

What the chief executive can do   There is more than enough evidence now that companies which have a high profile as regards social responsibility are generally more profitable than those which do not. Investment portfolios confined exclusively to companies which are perceived to be socially responsible usually perform better than the Stock Exchange average over the long term. The reason is partly that these companies are more sensitive and responsive to what is happening in world about them. This affects their whole strategy, so they are moving with society rather than against it.

Being a good corporate citizen requires an understanding of what is happening in society, and a sufficiently strong commitment to enlightened self-interest to be active rather than reactive on major social issues.

There are really two aspects of integrity towards the public. The first is an essentially negative one: not doing the host of things that are legally or socially unacceptable, from emitting pollution to giving bribes. The second is essentially positive and starts from the premise that the company that understands and responds to social issues can profit from them. A good example is the 3M company's '3P' programme (pollution prevention pays). During the late 1970s most companies in the chemical processing industry were claiming that expenditure on pollution control was a major drain on profitability. 3M, however, proved that smart planning and a little technological ingenuity could combine pollution prevention with waste prevention, thus making the whole a highly profitable exercise. As a result, more than 1000 individual projects in its plants around the world have saved it over $200 million in recovered materials and reduction in energy use.

It all boils down in the end to attitude. If you see fulfilling your company's social responsibilities as a necessary chore, rather than as an opportunity to maintain and expand its reputation, you are effectively limiting your flexibility to respond to what happens in the outside world. For this reason it pays to look at social requirements, particularly when backed by legislation, not as a nuisance to be dealt with at minimum cost but as a strategic opening. Spending excessive time and effort in trying to keep down the cost of adhering to social legislation, or in trying to avoid responsibilities, is like rowing upstream: the longer you go on, the harder work it seems to be. On the other hand it may often be more profitable to run with the stream, looking for ways in which you can capitalize on the spirit of the legislation.

Studies of what happens when a product comes under attack for health and safety reasons illustrate the point. The company with a strongly entrenched integrity ethic will immediately investigate to establish whether the danger is real. From the start it will involve both government agencies and environmentalists or other appropriate pressure groups. 'Let's try and establish the truth together' is the tone of the company's reaction. If joint or independent investigation establishes that the allegations are unfounded, it has already placed something of a moral obligation on the environmentalists and government agencies to lend their support to calming public fears.

A company which does not have a strong integrity ethic is more likely to adopt a tone of self-righteous indignation and dismiss the allegations as unwarranted and ill-informed. If it holds any dialogue on the issue with community opinion formers, this is of the most limited extent. The investigations it performs are likely to be half-hearted, to take longer and to reflect what middle managers assume top management wants to hear. Even if the product is, indeed, perfectly harmless, the company has a hard job convincing the public of the fact.

If the allegations do turn out to have some truth in them, then the behavioural gap between the two types of company widens even further. The low-integrity company procrastinates over when and how to remove the product from the market, having as its objective to keep the product alive as long as possible. It will typically release even less information, battening down the hatches as the storm of public disapproval grows. In the end, it is frequently forced to withdraw the product entirely. The opprobrium towards the one product gradually spreads to the company as a whole, affecting sales of *all* its products.

The high-integrity company admits its error immediately, and asks everyone concerned for ideas on how to overcome the problem. It may in extreme cases withdraw the product from sale straight away and embark upon a crash programme of R&D to replace it. At the very least it will give notice that it will resolve the problem within a given period of time. Such companies recognize that giving up a product is better than giving up a market. In many cases, it is possible to steal a substantial march on slower-moving, less socially responsive competition by beginning to design a safe replacement product as soon as it becomes clear that the problem may be real. Depending on the particular market, what began as a disaster may in fact turn out to be a significant opportunity to increase market share.

Another large part of integrity to the public is simply being a good neighbour. The way some companies treat their host community suggests that their top management is entirely composed of the sort of people who, in their own homes, play loud music late at night, run a part-time car-wrecking business in the front driveway and habitually light bonfires whenever a neighbour hangs out washing. In reality, of course, most of them are probably ideal domestic neighbours. Your answer to the question above, 'Would you like to live next door to one of your company's plants?', is a fundamental illustration of attitude towards the public. If the very idea of living there appals you, what opinion of your company must it generate among those people who *have* to live there? And how do you justify operating a double standard for behaviour in your own home and at work? If your company cares about its impact on the world outside, then it must at least do all it can to minimize the disturbance or damage it creates.

One of the most traumatic experiences a company can undergo is for an employee to blow the whistle on dishonest behaviour. As we write, the US firm General Dynamics is under investigation by the Department of Defense for alleged overcharging, as a result of one employee's attack of conscience. While your company may not deliberately intend to deceive or defraud, you would be among a very small minority of chief executives if you could truthfully say, 'No manager in my company is dealing dishonestly with the outside world.' Most illegal or dishonest behaviour in companies is carried out by dedicated managers whose behaviour outside the corporate fold is impeccable.

In most cases, these managers' companies either lack a consistent corporate code of ethics, or have a code which managers do not take seriously. These managers, usually in demanding jobs, lose contact with the real world and gradually adopt a set of moral values related solely to the success of their part of the business. Most would be horrified at the suggestion that what they were doing was immoral. Prosecution for their behaviour, if considered at all, comes to be viewed as just another business risk, and the assumption grows that should they be discovered, the company will stand by them because, after all, everything they are doing is on the company's behalf. Illegal price fixing, arrangement of 'sweeteners' and other criminal activities become acceptable practice.

Most such activities are never uncovered. But if you care about the integrity of your company and its reputation, you need to take active steps to minimize the likelihood of it happening. Among those steps are:

- establish a moral tone by your own example. Put business decisions into a social and moral as well as a financial and market context.
- open the issue of moral behaviour to discussion within the company. Don't bury examples of unacceptable behaviour; bring them into the open, show what you think about them and how you expect other people in the organization to feel about them.
- don't allow small groups of managers to become so isolated from the real world that they create their own morality. Encourage,

if not oblige, managers to take part in activities in the community at large, where they can maintain their moral equilibrium.

● open channels for whistleblowers to blow their whistles. Far better to have the issue investigated internally than for an employee to feel so frustrated that he goes to external authorities, such as the police or the Health and Safety Executive. The concept of the employee ombudsman mentioned above is a useful safety valve for such frustration, especially if he is able to refer concerns directly to top management.

● give your protection to employees who dissent. While you may not agree with what they say, as long as they do not become disruptive, their alternative view can be a valuable counterweight to the extremes of enthusiasm that sometimes blind managers to the drawbacks of their pet schemes. Some organizations go so far as to encourage a degree of constructive dissent. The US Nuclear Regulatory Commission, for example, has a regular award scheme for the best argued dissenting view by a professional employee.

What the individual manager can do   There are literally dozens of things the local unit manager can do to make his plant or office building a welcome guest. Some suggestions include:

● spend time talking to local institutions, for example giving career talks to schools

● help local schools and universities in the development of curricula that will increase the availability of suitable job candidates for your company

● allow local teachers to work in your operations to discover for themselves what business is really about

● invite the public in from time to time to see what you do and how important it is both to products or services they use and to the local economy

● try to minimize the nuisance to domestic neighbours. Consult them before you apply for planning permission for an extension; at this early stage they are more likely to give the proposal a rational hearing and to make practical suggestions.

● look for ways to help with local community problems. Could the Scouts use that old timber? Would the village hall be able to make use of some obsolete office furniture?

● try hard to maintain good relations with the local authority. It can make life a lot easier for you if they understand the needs of your business, and trust your good intentions towards the community.

These may all be small things, but they add together to create an impression of a company which cares about the community it lives in.

If you are a junior manager or supervisor, you can benefit both your company and your career by volunteering to represent the company at local events. Offer to take your superior's place in speaking to a school or voluntary society. Ask your subordinates for suggestions on how the company could be a better neighbour (some of them may actually live close by), and work any acceptable ideas up into proposals for your own superior. Above all, try to establish for yourself and your employees what is and what is not acceptable behaviour towards the community. Use the company code of ethics if there is one. If there isn't, talk to senior managers inside the firm and to opinion formers outside. (Your local clergy will probably have some strong views, as will many trade union officials.) Ask yourself, 'Is this the way I would wish to be treated?' You might even suggest to senior management that you take on the formal project of assembling the materials upon which a company code of ethics would be based. If nothing else, their reply will tell you something about the strength of their commitment to the integrity ethic.

Conclusion: Keep on winning

Of the forty-three US companies characterized as excellent by Peters and Waterman in their study, a third had slipped from their pedestal in the space of two years. At the time of writing only one of the companies we identified as having the winning streak – Barratt Developments – has fallen into serious problems, although the profit performance of most of the high-tech companies has dipped quite heavily, reflecting a general loss of lustre in the electronics sector around the world. It is, however, to be expected that over time a proportion of the best-run companies will lose their winning streak.

Does this mean that their formula for success was faulty? Did they really have the winning streak and, if not, what does that say about the common characteristics of successful businesses we identified from these companies?

As any top athlete knows, while it takes a great deal of hard work, determination and guts to get to the top, so too does staying there. The moment you slacken off, you are in danger of losing your edge. Staying excellent in all of the characteristics that bring success is like competing in a decathlon: only exceptional athletes participate at this level, but even so they are unlikely to be equally proficient across the whole range of activities in which they must compete. So it is with the winning streak. Tom Peters is quoted by *Business Week*, in an analysis of the fall from grace of some of the big names in *In Search of Excellence*, as saying 'that it is virtually impossible to score a perfect ten on all eight attributes of excellence' as identified in his study. That is a conclusion with which we would have to concur.

So where did the companies that lost their 'best run' status fall down? A few, such as Atari, says an article, 'Who's excellent now?' in *Business Week*,

> managed to break almost all of the eight commandments of excellence. Out-of-control management and bloated fiefdoms – not autonomy,

entrepreneurship, and a simple and lean form – were hallmarks at that company, whose payroll zoomed from a few hundred to 7000 and back to a few hundred in just seven years. Atari was so out of touch with its market that it failed to realize its customers were losing interest in video-game players and switching to home computers – a fatal oversight.

Indeed, *Business Week* identified that 'Of the 14 excellent companies that had stumbled, 12 were inept in adapting to a fundamental change in their market'. It went on to argue that the principles of excellence prevented these companies from being sensitive to and reacting to change in the outside world. That is not our experience with the 'winning streak' companies, for whom sensitivity to change in the world around them is a fundamental part of the management approach.

Another cause for decline identified by *Business Week* is that some excellent companies 'overstressed some attributes and ignored others'. They spent so much time preparing for the long jump they failed at the high jump. So how can your company or your department make sure that once it achieves the winning streak, it keeps it? We continue to believe that the most critical element is the quality of the leadership. The chief executive in particular must have drive, consistency, a long-term perspective – and the courage of his convictions. He must also know when to get out, when he no longer provides the quality of visionary leadership his company needs.

One suggestion for dealing with this problem at top management level is parliamentary management. Suggested by a Swedish academic some years ago, the concept revolves around competing boards of directors, one in power, the other paid to tour the world developing alternative programmes and strategies. As the board in power loses touch with the real world, the opposition is there to supplant it and bring about a return to reality. The potential difficulty with this kind of arrangement is that the company may be exposed to frequent changes of direction, as one board is voted off and another voted in. Competition for key senior and middle management jobs might also become even more politicized than it is at present. However, the general principle is of value: that top management needs a powerful alternative view to make sure the company does not become a victim of its own success.

There are less radical ways to maintain the winning streak than parliamentary management. For example:

- undertake regular, independent reviews of your company's or department's performance in terms of the 'winning streak' characteristics. These reviews may be of greatest value if carried out in parallel with the internal reviewing process. The biggest problems you face are likely to lie in the areas where the two reports differ most.

- listen to the 'still, small voice' at the back of your consciousness. All too often we dismiss tiny nagging doubts because we are afraid of where pursuing them might lead us. But you are not paid as a manager, and especially not as a chief executive, to avoid facing issues. Take a few minutes every day, if possible, to sit quietly and review all those things that you would rather not think about. Write them down, bring them out into the open, initiate investigation and analysis. If they prove groundless, you will be able to rest more easily at night; if they prove to be well founded, you will have tackled a problem before it becomes a crisis.

- watch for the signs of slackening off. If the rate of growth begins flattening out, is it because of market maturity or organizational maturity – i.e. are you and your team becoming fat cats? Has the number of customer complaints increased? Are previously sharp people allowing small errors to slip past them? Even the best, most dynamic teams begin to tire eventually. It is one sign of a good leader that he can spur them on again, start the adrenalin pumping once more.

- don't let the challenge wither. 'Having reached the top of the mountain, where is there to go but down?' is a subconscious attitude that has affected innumerable companies. Organizations that have exhibited the winning streak for a number of years, that have achieved dominance of the market sectors in which they operate, and that are conscious, even arrogant, of their organizational excellence can all too easily assume that others do not have the ability to catch up. Once your company or department has achieved a higher standard of excellence than its competitors, the 'winning streak' philosophy demands that, rather than accept this state as the natural order of things, you should seek to establish even higher levels, making it increasingly difficult for competitors to catch up. In other words, find a taller mountain.

- keep an eye on the balance between 'winning streak' characteristics. Maintain a chart that compares the strength of each characteristic in your company or department, and compares your performance with that of the competition. Define the competition in two ways and compare separately: first, those companies that compete in your narrow market sector; second, those that compete in the widest definition of your market. For example, if you are in the electronic instrumentation business, you should compare first with the people you sell against, then with the best companies in the electronics industry as a whole. In this way you will retain a broad perspective on your company and its comparative performance.

In ten years' time, the list of British companies most clearly exhibiting the winning streak will almost certainly have undergone some change, although we suspect that a majority of the current names will still be there. By the law of averages and by the simple fact that even the best companies can sometimes end up with a less than outstanding leader, a certain number will inevitably fall by the wayside.

If we come to write a follow-up book at that time, we believe there will be valuable lessons in the experiences of those companies that *lost* the winning streak, and how they did so. Among the new crop of successful arrivals, we are sure there will also be examples of companies that have consciously set out to achieve the winning streak by consciously developing excellence in leadership, autonomy, control, involvement, market orientation, zero basing, innovation and integrity.

We hope yours will be among them.

Appendix:
The development of the mature entrepreneurial company

Most companies start with an entrepreneur, who takes the organization through early, swift growth. He normally operates with few controls and a great deal of flexibility.

Eventually, if the company survives, it requires the professional management of the 'consolidator' or co-ordinator, who introduces controls and systems. In doing so he frequently rationalizes the disparate elements of the entrepreneur's empire. If he does his job well, the controls he introduces underwrite the entrepreneurial spirit of the empire. All too often, however, he opts for centralization and the gradual buildup of bureaucracy. Once that buildup begins, like the fatty deposits on the walls of an ailing artery, it progressively constricts the flow of information, imagination and initiative.

A major crisis may force the company to slice away some of the bureaucracy, but by then the organization structure is too rigid for the effect to be permanent or pervasive. It is rather like the heart patient giving up fatty foods and smoking, yet still not being able to run up stairs. To instil real changes in attitude and behaviour, the organization itself must be changed until it regains something of the entrepreneurial spirit it started with. To do this requires a 'network maker' who takes the organized, relatively mature organization and attempts to rekindle the enthusiasm, growth and sense of mission that was apparent in the entrepreneurial stage. He relaxes controls, decentralizes and experiments.

Guiding the organization between any or all of these stages may be the transitional leader. This may also be the person who leads the company out of crisis. His role is as an agent of change, and he may well be a misfit in the organization when that change is accomplished. Sir Michael Edwardes is an interesting example. He has achieved his success primarily as a 'company doctor' rather than as a long-term leader. He is perhaps well described as a wandering knight, always willing to come to the aid of companies in distress, but not a permanent companion.

By and large, the long-established 'winning streak' companies have emerged into or are in transition to the third stage of leadership. They have broken through the staidness of corporate middle age to the second vitality of the decentralized, flexible organization. Some of the younger companies appear to have made the transition without suffering the traumas of middle age or maturity at all; they have moved directly from entrepreneurial leadership to network-maker leadership and their organizations have evolved accordingly. We believe that the ability of today's entrepreneurial business to make that same direct transition will be a significant factor in the growth of the British economy in the 1990s. The more companies, both entrepreneurial and mature, that can achieve the transition to a decentralized, semi-autonomous network, the greater will be the vitality of the industrial and business economy as a whole.

What we are describing here is of far more significance than the swings between centralization and decentralization that have characterized business fashion in Europe and the United States over the past fifty years. It is a fundamental commitment to preserving the entrepreneurial spirit within large and complex organizations. One possible development we are already beginning to see in embryo is what we might describe as the European *zaibatsu*, the Japanese term for organizations where a large company, through a series of buyouts, joint ventures and special relationships with both suppliers and former employees who have left to start their own businesses, finds itself as the nexus of a broadly based industrial club. Membership of the club is likely to be based both on the informal criterion of shared management philosophies and on the formal criterion of mutual minority ownership. The movement of employees at all levels between the different independent companies will be much easier than in the normal business world; intertrading will be high; and companies within the club will come to each other's aid in times of trouble. Gradually, the original large company may become just one of several major nodes in the network.

If this all seems fanciful, look at the current development of Rank Xerox. Not only are significant numbers of employees now working as independent suppliers – some of them rapidly expanding into sizeable businesses – but Rank Xerox has also dispersed its field sales operations into an *ad hoc* mixture of directly owned subsidiaries, joint ventures and independent franchises. Many of the employees, including the chairman, now work part of the time from home via computer and telephone line. The pattern of heavy central control has given way to organized autonomy.

Bibliography

Creating Commitment in Project-Based Industries, British Institute of Management one-day conference, London, February 1985

Delivering the Goods, Department of Industry, London, 1983

'Leading change by changing maps', *Boston Consulting Group Annual Perspective*, 1984

Managing for Innovation, British Institute of Management, London, November 1984

'The new breed of strategic planner', *Business Week*, McGraw-Hill, New York, September 1984

'Today's thorniest management problem: new technology', *International Management*, Maidenhead, December 1984

'Who's excellent now?', *Business Week*, McGraw-Hill, New York, November 1984

William J. Abernathy, Kim B. Clark, Alan M. Kantrow, *Industrial Renaissance*, Basic Books, New York, 1983

John Adair, *Effective Leadership*, Gower, Aldershot, 1983

Frederick D. Buggie, *New Product Development Strategies*, AMACOM, New York, 1981

Irving G. Calish, 'The challenge of internal corporate venturing', *SAM Advanced Management Journal*, Autumn 1984

Graham Cleverley, *Managers and Magic*, Penguin Books, Harmondsworth, 1971

David Clutterbuck, *How to Be a Good Corporate Citizen*, McGraw-Hill, Maidenhead, 1981

David Clutterbuck and Roy Hill, *The Re-Making of Work*, Grant McIntyre, London, 1981

Gordon Donaldson and Jay W. Lorsch, *Decision Making at the Top*, Basic Books, New York, 1983

Michiel Fischer and Kees Blokland, *The Dangers of Too Much Excellence*, Paper to British Institute of Management conference, London, 1984

Lawrence G. Franko, *The Threat of Japanese Multinationals – How the West Can Respond*, John Wiley & Sons, Chichester, 1983

David A. Garvin, 'What does "product quality" really mean?', *Sloan Management Review*, Cambridge, Mass, Fall 1984, Vol 26 No 1

Walter Goldsmith and David Clutterbuck, *The Winning Streak*, Weidenfeld & Nicolson, London, 1984

Jay Hall, *The Competence Process*, Telemetrics International, Texas, 1980

Geert Hofstede, 'Motivation, leadership, and organization: do American theories apply abroad?', *Organizational Dynamics*, AMACOM, New York, 1980

Daniel J. Isenberg, 'How senior managers think', *Harvard Business Review*, Cambridge, Mass, November–December 1984

J. H. Jackson and C. P. Morgan, *Organization Theory: A Macro Perspective for Management*, Prentice-Hall, New Jersey, 1982

Kono, *Strategy and Structure of Japanese Enterprises*, Macmillan, London, 1985

Jean-Claude Larreche, Nick Hamel-Smith and Volney Stefflre, 'New life in old markets', *Issues: The PA Journal for Management*, London, Vol 2 No 1, 1985

Theodore Levitt, 'The marketing imagination', *Harvard Business School Bulletin*, December 1983

Christopher Lorenz, 'Marketing myopia: an insidious disease', *Financial Times*, London, April 1985

Alistair Mant, *Leaders We Deserve*, Martin Robertson, Oxford, 1983

Judi Marshall and Adrian McLean, *Current Research in Management*, Frances Pinter, London, April 1985

Michael E. Naylor, 'Regaining your competitive edge', *Long Range Planning*, London, February 1985

R. C. Parker, *Going for Growth*, John Wiley & Sons, Chichester, 1985

Richard Pearson, Rosemary Hutt and David Parsons, *Education, Training and Employment*, Gower, Aldershot, 1984

Thomas J. Peters and Robert H. Waterman Jr., *In Search of Excellence*, Harper & Row, New York, 1982

Nigel Piercy, *Export Strategy: Markets and Competition*, George Allen & Unwin, London, 1982

Michael E. Porter, *Competition in Global Industries: A Conceptual Framework*, Harvard Business School, 1984

David A. Ricks and Vijay Mahajan, 'Blunders in international marketing: fact or fiction', *International Journal of Strategic and Long Range Planning*, London, Vol. 17 No. 1, February 1984

Elaine Romanelli and Michael L. Tushman, *Executive Leadership and Organizational Outcomes: An Evolutionary Perspective*, Columbia University, New York, 1983

Graham Saunders, *The Committed Organisation*, Gower, Aldershot, 1984

Wickham Skinner, 'Re-inventing the factory', *Issues: The PA Journal for Management*, London, Vol. 1 No. 2, 1984

Robert E. Spekman, 'Competitive procurement strategies: building strength and reducing vulnerability', *International Journal of Strategic and Long Range Planning*, Henley Management College, February 1985

Noel M. Tichy and David O. Ulrich, 'The leadership challenge – a call for the transformational leader', *Sloan Management Review*, Cambridge, Mass, Fall 1984, Vol 26 No 1

Benjamin Tregoe and John Zimmerman, *Top Management Strategy*, John Martin, London, 1980

Michael L. Tushman and Elaine Romanelli, *Organizational Evolution: A Metamorphosis Model of Convergence and Reorientation*, Columbia University, New York, November 1983

John Walmsley, *Handbook of International Joint Ventures*, Graham and Trotman, London, 1982

MORE ABOUT PENGUINS, PELICANS, PEREGRINES AND PUFFINS

For further information about books available from Penguins please write to Dept EP, Penguin Books Ltd, Harmondsworth, Middlesex UB7 0DA.

In the U.S.A.: For a complete list of books available from Penguins in the United States write to Dept DG, Penguin Books, 299 Murray Hill Parkway, East Rutherford, New Jersey 07073.

In Canada: For a complete list of books available from Penguins in Canada write to Penguin Books Canada Ltd, 2801 John Street, Markham, Ontario L3R 1B4.

In Australia: For a complete list of books available from Penguins in Australia write to the Marketing Department, Penguin Books Australia Ltd, P.O. Box 257, Ringwood, Victoria 3134.

In New Zealand: For a complete list of books available from Penguins in New Zealand write to the Marketing Department, Penguin Books (N.Z.) Ltd, Private Bag, Takapuna, Auckland 9.

In India: For a complete list of books available from Penguins in India write to Penguin Overseas Ltd, 706 Eros Apartments, 56 Nehru Place, New Delhi 110019.

A CHOICE OF PENGUINS

☐ *The Complete Penguin Stereo Record and Cassette Guide*
Greenfield, Layton and March   £7.95

A new edition, now including information on compact discs. 'One of the few indispensables on the record collector's bookshelf' – *Gramophone*

☐ *Selected Letters of Malcolm Lowry*
Edited by Harvey Breit and Margerie Bonner Lowry £5.95

'Lowry emerges from these letters not only as an extremely interesting man, but also a lovable one' – Philip Toynbee

☐ *The First Day on the Somme*
Martin Middlebrook   £3.95

1 July 1916 was the blackest day of slaughter in the history of the British Army. 'The soldiers receive the best service a historian can provide: their story told in their own words' – *Guardian*

☐ *A Better Class of Person* **John Osborne**   £2.50

The playwright's autobiography, 1929–56. 'Splendidly enjoyable' – John Mortimer. 'One of the best, richest and most bitterly truthful autobiographies that I have ever read' – Melvyn Bragg

☐ *The Winning Streak* **Goldsmith and Clutterbuck**   £2.95

Marks & Spencer, Saatchi & Saatchi, United Biscuits, GEC ... The UK's top companies reveal their formulas for success, in an important and stimulating book that no British manager can afford to ignore.

☐ *The First World War* **A. J. P. Taylor**   £4.95

'He manages in some 200 illustrated pages to say almost everything that is important ... A special text ... a remarkable collection of photographs' – *Observer*

A CHOICE OF PENGUINS

☐ *Man and the Natural World* **Keith Thomas** £4.95

Changing attitudes in England, 1500–1800. 'An encyclopedic study of man's relationship to animals and plants . . . a book to read again and again' – Paul Theroux, *Sunday Times* Books of the Year

☐ *Jean Rhys: Letters 1931–66*
   Edited by Francis Wyndham and Diana Melly £4.95

'Eloquent and invaluable . . . her life emerges, and with it a portrait of an unexpectedly indomitable figure' – Marina Warner in the *Sunday Times*

☐ *The French Revolution* **Christopher Hibbert** £4.95

'One of the best accounts of the Revolution that I know . . . Mr Hibbert is outstanding' – J. H. Plumb in the *Sunday Telegraph*

☐ *Isak Dinesen* **Judith Thurman** £4.95

The acclaimed life of Karen Blixen, 'beautiful bride, disappointed wife, radiant lover, bereft and widowed woman, writer, sibyl, Scheherazade, child of Lucifer, Baroness; always a unique human being . . . an assiduously researched and finely narrated biography' – *Books & Bookmen*

☐ *The Amateur Naturalist*
   Gerald Durrell with Lee Durrell £4.95

'Delight . . . on every page . . . packed with authoritative writing, learning without pomposity . . . it represents a real bargain' – *The Times Educational Supplement*. 'What treats are in store for the average British household' – *Daily Express*

☐ *When the Wind Blows* **Raymond Briggs** £2.95

'A visual parable against nuclear war: all the more chilling for being in the form of a strip cartoon' – *Sunday Times*. 'The most eloquent anti-Bomb statement you are likely to read' – *Daily Mail*

A CHOICE OF
PELICANS AND PEREGRINES

A CHOICE OF
PELICANS AND PEREGRINES

PENGUIN REFERENCE BOOKS

☐ **The Penguin Map of the World**   £2.95

Clear, colourful, crammed with information and fully up-to-date, this is a useful map to stick on your wall at home, at school or in the office.

☐ **The Penguin Map of Europe**   £2.95

Covers all land eastwards to the Urals, southwards to North Africa and up to Syria, Iraq and Iran * Scale = 1:5,500,000 * 4-colour artwork * Features main roads, railways, oil and gas pipelines, plus extra information including national flags, currencies and populations.

☐ **The Penguin Map of the British Isles**   £2.95

Including the Orkneys, the Shetlands, the Channel Islands and much of Normandy, this excellent map is ideal for planning routes and touring holidays, or as a study aid.

☐ **The Penguin Dictionary of Quotations**   £3.95

A treasure-trove of over 12,000 new gems and old favourites, from Aesop and Matthew Arnold to Xenophon and Zola.

☐ **The Penguin Dictionary of Art and Artists**   £3.95

Fifth Edition. 'A vast amount of information intelligently presented, carefully detailed, abreast of current thought and scholarship and easy to read' – *The Times Literary Supplement*

☐ **The Penguin Pocket Thesaurus**   £2.50

A pocket-sized version of Roget's classic, and an essential companion for all commuters, crossword addicts, students, journalists and the stuck-for-words.

PENGUIN REFERENCE BOOKS

☐ *The Penguin Dictionary of Troublesome Words*   £2.50

A witty, straightforward guide to the pitfalls and hotly disputed issues in standard written English, illustrated with examples and including a glossary of grammatical terms and an appendix on punctuation.

☐ *The Penguin Guide to the Law*   £8.95

This acclaimed reference book is designed for everyday use, and forms the most comprehensive handbook ever published on the law as it affects the individual.

☐ *The Penguin Dictionary of Religions*   £4.95

The rites, beliefs, gods and holy books of all the major religions throughout the world are covered in this book, which is illustrated with charts, maps and line drawings.

☐ *The Penguin Medical Encyclopedia*   £4.95

Covers the body and mind in sickness and in health, including drugs, surgery, history, institutions, medical vocabulary and many other aspects. Second Edition. 'Highly commendable' – *Journal of the Institute of Health Education*

☐ *The Penguin Dictionary of Physical Geography*   £4.95

This book discusses all the main terms used, in over 5,000 entries illustrated with diagrams and meticulously cross-referenced.

☐ *Roget's Thesaurus*   £3.50

Specially adapted for Penguins, Sue Lloyd's acclaimed new version of Roget's original will help you find the right words for your purposes. 'As normal a part of an intelligent household's library as the Bible, Shakespeare or a dictionary' – *Daily Telegraph*